Primary Source Accounts of
World War II

JOHN RICHARD CONWAY, ESQ.

MyReportLinks.com Books

an imprint of

 Enslow Publishers, Inc. E

Box 398, 40 Industrial Road

MyReportLinks.com Books, an imprint of Enslow Publishers, Inc. MyReportLinks®
is a registered trademark of Enslow Publishers, Inc.

Library of Congress Cataloging-in-Publication Data

Conway, John Richard, 1969–
  Primary source accounts of World War II / John Richard Conway.
     p. cm. — (America's wars through primary sources)
  Includes bibliographical references and index.
  ISBN 1-59845-002-6
  1. World War, 1939–1945—Juvenile literature. I. Title. II. Series.
  D743.7.C67 2006
  940.53—dc22

                                    2006000214

Printed in the United States of America

10 9 8 7 6 5 4 3 2 1

To Our Readers:
Through the purchase of this book, you and your library gain access to the Report Links that specifically
back up this book.
The Publisher will provide access to the Report Links that back up this book and will keep these Report
Links up to date on **www.myreportlinks.com** for five years from the book's first publication date.
We have done our best to make sure all Internet addresses in this book were active and appropriate when
we went to press. However, the author and the Publisher have no control over, and assume no liability
for, the material available on those Internet sites or on other Web sites they may link to.
The usage of the MyReportLinks.com Books Web site is subject to the terms and conditions stated on the
Usage Policy Statement on **www.myreportlinks.com**.
A password may be required to access the Report Links that back up this book. The password is found
on the bottom of page 4 of this book.
Any comments or suggestions can be sent by e-mail to comments@myreportlinks.com or to the address
on the back cover.

Photo Credits: British Broadcasting Corporation, p. 34; Calvin College, p. 19; Dwight D. Eisenhower
Presidential Library, p. 40; Enslow Publishers, p. 8; Franklin D. Roosevelt Presidential Library and
Museum, p. 52; Joseph Steinbacher Collection (AFC/2001/001/1883), Veterans History Project,
American Folklife Center, Library of Congress, p. 72; Library of Congress, pp. 11, 30, 36, 46, 55, 80, 95,
97, 100; Marie Voltzke Collection (AFC/2001/001/2884), Veterans History Project, American Folklife
Center, Library of Congress, p. 75; MyReportLinks.com Books, p. 4; National Archives and Records
Administration, pp. 60, 77, 92, 93, 99, 102, 107, 110; National Archives and Records
Administration/Department of Defense, pp. 1, 3, 9, 17, 21, 24, 27, 29, 32, 37, 44, 53, 57, 58, 62, 66, 70,
84, 88, 90; National World War II Memorial, p. 114; New Mexico State University, p. 50; Northwestern
University Library, p. 12; PBS, pp. 39, 43, 68; Smithsonian Institution, pp. 79, 106; The Center for World
War II Studies & Conflict Resolution at Brookdale Community College, p. 112; The Gilder Lehrman
Institute of American History, p. 63; The National Archives of the United Kingdom, p. 86; The University
of Missouri and the Truman Presidential Museum and Library, p. 14; University of Northern Iowa, p. 15;
University of Texas, p. 22; Veterans Museum and Memorial Center, p. 105; Yale Law School, p. 48.

Cover Photo: General Dwight D. Eisenhower speaks to paratroopers in England before they board
planes to be dropped behind enemy lines in France in the first assault of the D-Day invasion, June 6,
1944; National Archives and Records Administration/The Department of Defense.

Every effort has been made to locate all copyright holders of material used in this book. If any errors or
omissions have occurred, please contact us at www.myreportlinks.com. We will try to make corrections
in future editions.

CONTENTS

MyReportLinks.com Books
Great Books, Great Links, Great for Research!

The Internet sites featured in this book can save you hours of research time. These Internet sites—we call them **"Report Links"**—are constantly changing, but we keep them up to date on our Web site.

When you see this "Approved Web Site" logo, you will know that we are directing you to a great Internet site that will help you with your research.

Give it a try! Type http://www.myreportlinks.com into your browser, click on the series title and enter the password, then click on the book title, and scroll down to the Report Links listed for this book.

The Report Links will bring you to great source documents, photographs, and illustrations. MyReportLinks.com Books save you time, feature Report Links that are kept up to date, and make report writing easier than ever! A complete listing of the Report Links can be found on pages 116–117 at the back of the book.

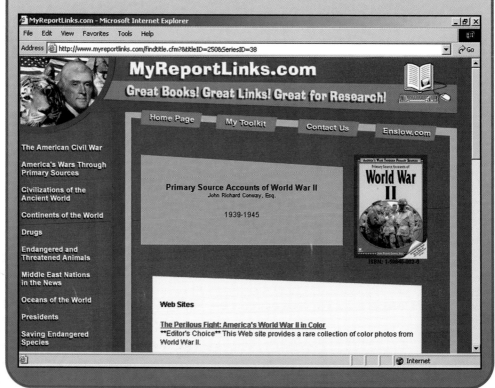

Please see "To Our Readers" on the copyright page for important information about this book, the MyReportLinks.com Web site, and the Report Links that back up this book.

Please enter **PWT1240** if asked for a password.

WHAT ARE PRIMARY SOURCES?

July 25, 1944.

I can't believe, Junie, that men will always have to fight. Men don't always have to fight. They detest it. And if they didn't when they came, they learned to damn quickly.

—Letter from Lieutenant Tracy A. Sugarman to his wife.[1]

The soldier who wrote these words never dreamed that they would be read by anyone but his wife. They were not intended to be read as a history of World War II. But his words—and the words of others that have come down to us through scholars or were saved over generations by family members—are unique resources. Historians call such writings primary source documents. As you read this book, you will find other primary source accounts of the war written by the men and women who fought it. Their letters home reflect their thoughts, their dreams, their fears, and their longing for loved ones. Some of them speak of the excitement of battle, while others mention the everyday boredom of day-to-day life in camp.

But the story of a war is not only the story of the men and women in service. This book also contains diary entries, newspaper accounts, official documents, and speeches of the war years. They reflect the opinions of those who were not in battle but who were still affected by the war. All of these things as well as photographs and art are primary sources—they were created by people who participated in, witnessed, or were affected by the events of the time.

Many of these sources, such as letters and diaries, are a reflection of personal experience. Others, such as newspaper accounts, reflect the mood of the time as well as the opinions of the papers' editors. All of them give us a unique insight into history as it happened. But it is also important to keep in mind that each source reflects its author's biases, beliefs, and background. Each is still someone's interpretation of an event.

Some of the primary sources in this book will be easy to understand; others may not. Their authors came from a different time and were products of different backgrounds and levels of education. So as you read their words, you will see that some of those words may be spelled differently than we would spell them. And some of their stories may be written without the kinds of punctuation we are used to seeing. Each source has been presented as it was originally written, but wherever a word or phrase is unclear or might be misunderstood, an explanation has been added.

TIME LINE OF WORLD WAR II

1939 —SEPTEMBER 1: Germany invades Poland.

—SEPTEMBER 3: France and Great Britain declare war on Germany.

—SEPTEMBER 17: The Soviet Union invades Poland.

1940 —APRIL 9: Germany invades Denmark and Norway.

—MAY 10: Neville Chamberlain resigns as British prime minister; Winston Churchill becomes prime minister. Germany invades France, Belgium, the Netherlands, and Luxembourg.

—MAY 26: The beginning of Operation Dynamo, the evacuation of Dunkirk.

—JUNE 10: Italy declares war on France and Great Britain.

—JUNE 22: France surrenders to Germany.

—JUNE 24: Japanese troops land in French Indochina.

—JULY 10: The Battle of Britain begins.

—SEPTEMBER 27: Germany, Japan, and Italy sign the Tripartite Agreement.

—SEPTEMBER 28: Italy invades Greece.

1941 —FEBRUARY 12: General Rommel arrives in Tripoli with the German Afrika Korps.

—APRIL 6: Germany invades Greece and Yugoslavia.

—JUNE 22: Operation Barbarossa—Germany invades the Soviet Union.

—DECEMBER 7: Japan attacks the United States at Pearl Harbor.

—DECEMBER 8: The United States declares war on Japan; three days later, it declares war on Germany and Italy.

—DECEMBER 11: Germany and Italy declare war on the United States.

—DECEMBER 14: Japan invades Burma.

—DECEMBER 24: Japanese military captures Wake Island.

1942 —FEBRUARY 15: Singapore surrenders to the Japanese.

—APRIL 9: American forces surrender to Japanese forces on Bataan, in the Philippines.

—APRIL 18: Doolittle Raid on Tokyo.

—MAY 5: Battle of Coral Sea begins.

—MAY 6: American forces at Corregidor surrender.

—JUNE 4: Battle of Midway Island begins.

—JUNE 20: Rommel and the Afrika Korps take Tobruk.

—JULY 12: Fighting around Stalingrad begins.

—AUGUST 7: American forces attack the Solomon Islands.

—AUGUST 8: Battle of Savo Island begins.

—AUGUST 19: Commando assault on Dieppe.

—SEPTEMBER 17: Japanese advance stopped on Guadalcanal.

—OCTOBER 23: Second Battle for El Alamein begins.

—NOVEMBER 8: Operation Torch: American troops land in North Africa.

1943 —FEBRUARY 2: German forces at Stalingrad surrender.

—FEBRUARY 14: Battle of Kasserine Pass.

—MAY 13: Axis troops in Tunisia surrender.

—JULY 10: Allied forces invade Sicily.

—JULY 25: Italian dictator Benito Mussolini is overthrown.

—AUGUST 17: Axis troops surrender in Sicily.

—SEPTEMBER 3: Allies invade Italy.

—NOVEMBER 20: American forces invade Tarawa.

—NOVEMBER 28: Teheran Conference begins.

1944 —JANUARY 3: Battle for Cassino begins.

—JANUARY 27: German siege of Leningrad ends.

—JANUARY 31: American forces invade the Marshall Islands.

—MAY 18: Cassino falls.

—JUNE 4: Rome is captured by the Allies.

—JUNE 6: D-Day landings at Normandy.

—JUNE 15: Americans invade Saipan.

—JUNE 19: Battle of the Philippine Sea begins.

—JULY 3: Minsk recaptured by Soviet forces.

—JULY 21: American forces invade Guam.

—JULY 30: Japanese withdraw from Burma.

—AUGUST 15: Allied invasion of the south of France.

—SEPTEMBER 15: American forces invade the Palau Islands.

—SEPTEMBER 17: Operation Market Garden begins.

—OCTOBER 10: American forces attack Okinawa.

—OCTOBER 23: The Battle of Leyte Gulf begins.

—DECEMBER 16: The Battle of the Bulge begins.

1945 —JANUARY 9: American forces land in Luzon, the Philippines.

—JANUARY 17: The Red Army (the army of the Soviet Union) enters Warsaw.

—FEBRUARY 19: American forces land in Iwo Jima.

—MARCH 9: Firebomb attack on Tokyo.

—MARCH 22: American forces cross the Rhine River.

—APRIL 24: Soviet forces enter the Berlin suburbs.

—APRIL 30: Hitler commits suicide.

—MAY 2: Berlin surrenders to Soviet forces.

—MAY 7: Germany signs an unconditional surrender.

—JULY 17: Potsdam Conference.

—AUGUST 6: The United States drops the atomic bomb on Hiroshima.

—AUGUST 9: The United States drops another atomic bomb, this time on Nagasaki.

—AUGUST 15: Japanese forces surrender.

—SEPTEMBER 2: Japanese sign armistice in Tokyo Bay, ending World War II.

European Theater 1944–1945

Atlantic Ocean

SCOTLAND

IRELAND

ENGLAND

North Sea

NORWAY

SWEDEN

DENMARK

Baltic Sea

Hamburg

Elbe R.

NETHERLANDS

Berlin

London

Dunkirk

Antwerp

Calais

BELGIUM

English Channel

Le Havre

GERMANY

Prague

Normandy Invasion

LUX.

Paris

Battle of the Bulge

Moselle R.

CZECHOSLOVAKIA

Seine R.

NAZI OCCUPIED ZONE

Loire R.

Rhine R.

Danube R.

Munich

Atlantic Ocean

SWITZERLAND

AUSTRIA

Bay of Biscay

FRANCE

Lyon

ITALY

Adriatic Sea

Rhône R.

Marseille

Mediterranean Sea

SPAIN

KEY

- Normandy Invasion
- Allied Drive to the Rhine
- Capital
- Cities
- Battles
- Border

Pacific Theater 1941–1945

Sea of Japan

KOREA

JAPAN

Tokyo

Hiroshima

Nagasaki

CHINA

Okinawa

Volcano Islands

Iwo Jima

Pacific Ocean

Midway

FORMOSA

Hong Kong

Philippine Sea

Wake Island

Pearl Harbor

HAWAIIAN ISLANDS

South China Sea

Bataan

Manila

Philippine Sea

Mariana Islands

Saipan

Tinian

Guam

Johnston Island

PHILIPPINES

Leyte Gulf

Peleliu

Palau Islands

Caroline Islands

Marshall Islands

Singapore

Gilbert Islands

Tarawa

DUTCH BORNEO

NETHERLANDS EAST INDIES

JAVA

NEW GUINEA

Rabaul

New Britain

Solomon Islands

Guadalcanal

Coral Sea

▲ The main European and Pacific theaters of war in World War II after the United States became involved.

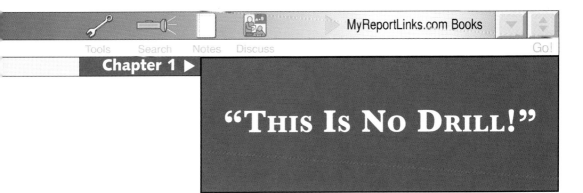
"THIS IS NO DRILL!"

Early on the morning of December 7, 1941, the American fleet stationed at Pearl Harbor was nearly destroyed by Japanese carrier-based bombers. The Japanese had sent a large fleet of six aircraft carriers to destroy the United States fleet, the Navy's group of warships, to give the Japanese time to strike

▲ A photograph captured from the Japanese shows an enemy bomber's view of the attack on Pearl Harbor. The attack brought America into World War II.

south. The Japanese lost twenty-nine airplanes that day, but the U.S. fleet lost six battleships, three cruisers, three destroyers, and several other ships. It was a crippling blow to the United States Navy's offensive capabilities, but it was not the knock-out punch the Japanese had hoped for. The dockyards and oil facilities were mostly untouched, allowing the U.S. Navy to continue to use Hawaii as a staging post. The Navy's carriers and several cruisers were not present at Pearl Harbor during the attack, so they escaped destruction.

Lee Soucy, a crewman on the battleship USS *Utah,* was going through his normal morning routine that Sunday morning when the ship was attacked by three aerial torpedoes and was sunk.

> After I bobbed up to the surface of the water to get my bearings, I spotted a motor launch with a coxswain fishing men out of the water with his boat hook. I started to swim toward the launch. After a few strokes, a hail of bullets hit the water a few feet in front of me in line with the launch. As the strafer banked, I noticed the big red insignias on his wingtips. Until then, I really had not known who attacked us. At some point, I had heard someone shout, "Where did those Germans come from?"[1]

Soucy's question about "those Germans" referred to the Nazi regime in Germany and its military, which had been waging war in Europe since 1939. But it was the Japanese, not the Germans, who

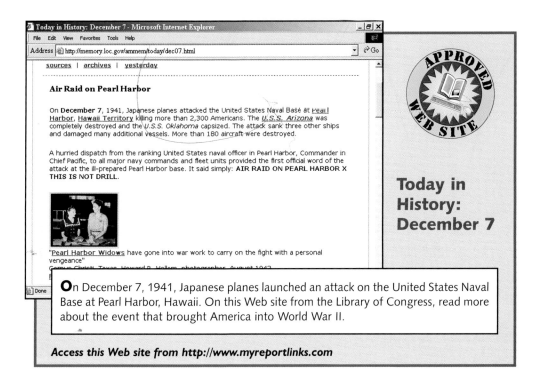

Today in History: December 7 - Microsoft Internet Explorer

File   Edit   View   Favorites   Tools   Help

Address   http://memory.loc.gov/ammem/today/dec07.html   Go

sources | archives | yesterday

Air Raid on Pearl Harbor

On **December 7, 1941**, Japanese planes attacked the United States Naval Base at Pearl Harbor, Hawaii Territory killing more than 2,300 Americans. The U.S.S. Arizona was completely destroyed and the U.S.S. Oklahoma capsized. The attack sank three other ships and damaged many additional vessels. More than 180 aircraft were destroyed.

A hurried dispatch from the ranking United States naval officer in Pearl Harbor, Commander in Chief Pacific, to all major navy commands and fleet units provided the first official word of the attack at the ill-prepared Pearl Harbor base. It said simply: AIR RAID ON PEARL HARBOR X THIS IS NOT DRILL.

"Pearl Harbor Widows have gone into war work to carry on the fight with a personal vengeance"
Corpus Christi, Texas, Howard R. Hollem, photographer, August 1942

Today in History: December 7

On December 7, 1941, Japanese planes launched an attack on the United States Naval Base at Pearl Harbor, Hawaii. On this Web site from the Library of Congress, read more about the event that brought America into World War II.

Access this Web site from http://www.myreportlinks.com

launched the surprise attack on Pearl Harbor, Hawaii, that December morning. (Hawaii was a United States territory at the time; it would not become a state until 1959.) That attack brought America into World War II, the most devastating war in human history. The Japanese managed to cause a great deal of destruction on the U.S. fleet, but the surprised Americans fought back with vigor.

▷ "Praise the Lord and Pass the Ammunition!"

Andy Gura, a naval reservist serving on the USS *New Orleans,* recalls his experience the morning of the attack, especially the words of a chaplain on board ship. Those words were immortalized in song.

When we spotted those meatballs [the Japanese planes] the thing for us to do was go to our battle stations. We got our five-inchers [large mounted guns] and our machine guns going in a big hurry. I really don't know for sure if we hit anything or not. I do remember watching some Japanese planes going down that we had been firing at.

Our ship's chaplain was an officer named Howell M. Forgy. When he heard General Quarters, he ran over to our five-inchers. The men had set up a chain gang passing up the ammunition. The Chaplain saw this and he shouted, "Praise the Lord and pass the ammunition." And whenever they'd slack off, he'd yell again, "Praise

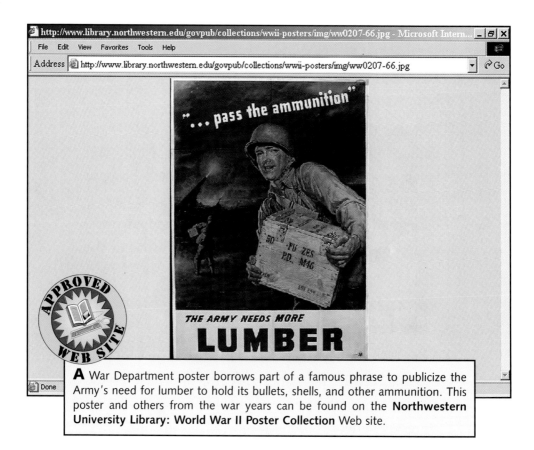

A War Department poster borrows part of a famous phrase to publicize the Army's need for lumber to hold its bullets, shells, and other ammunition. This poster and others from the war years can be found on the **Northwestern University Library: World War II Poster Collection** Web site.

the Lord and pass the ammunition." This went on until the second wave of Japanese planes had passed.

Well, you can bet it spread through the fleet how a sky pilot [the chaplain] had been the cheerleader for the gunners on the New Orleans.[2]

Amid the wreckage and confusion, the Americans' spirit of defiance was evident. A Japanese pilot involved in the attack witnessed such determination.

I was diving down to take another run at Ewa (Marine Airfield). We had already bombed the hell out of the place. I saw this one American, standing next to a disabled plane. He just stood there, firing and reloading his pistol. He didn't give an inch. He was truly a Yankee samurai.[3]

Admiral Isoroku Yamamoto, the Japanese architect of the attack on Pearl Harbor, was remarkably perceptive when he told his cheering junior officers, "Gentlemen, I'm afraid all we have done is awaken a sleeping giant and filled him with a terrible resolve."[4]

▶ "A Date Which Will Live in Infamy"

On December 8, 1941, the day following the attacks, President Franklin Delano Roosevelt addressed Congress with words that have now become famous:

Yesterday, 7 December 1941—a date which will live in infamy—the United States of America was suddenly

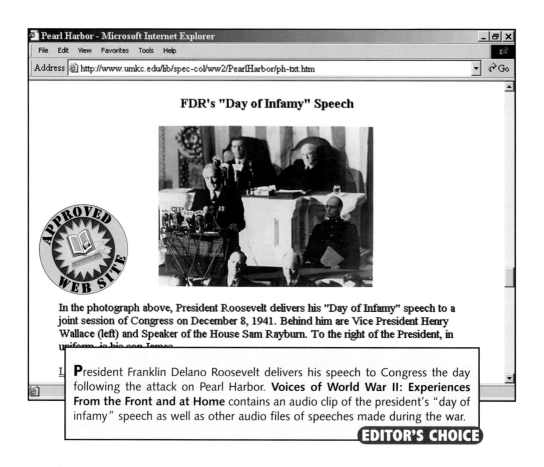

FDR's "Day of Infamy" Speech

In the photograph above, President Roosevelt delivers his "Day of Infamy" speech to a joint session of Congress on December 8, 1941. Behind him are Vice President Henry Wallace (left) and Speaker of the House Sam Rayburn. To the right of the President, in uniform, is his son James.

President Franklin Delano Roosevelt delivers his speech to Congress the day following the attack on Pearl Harbor. **Voices of World War II: Experiences From the Front and at Home** contains an audio clip of the president's "day of infamy" speech as well as other audio files of speeches made during the war.

and deliberately attacked by naval and air forces of the Empire of Japan. . . .

Roosevelt ended the speech with these words:

I ask that the Congress declare that since the unprovoked and dastardly attack by Japan on Sunday, Dec. 7, a state of war has existed between the United States and the Japanese empire.[5]

With those words, the United States of America entered World War II.

Chapter 2

A BRIEF HISTORY OF THE WAR IN EUROPE

The origins of World War II arose from the end of World War I. The Treaty of Versailles that ended World War I blamed the war directly on Germany even though the war started on the Balkan Peninsula. Germany paid enormous amounts of money in reparations, or compensation, to the nations it had invaded, and lost enormous amounts of territory.

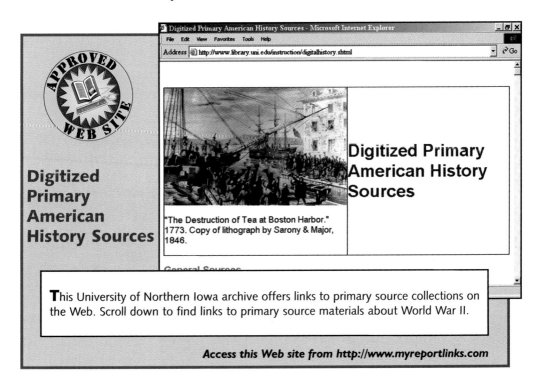

Digitized Primary American History Sources

Digitized Primary American History Sources - Microsoft Internet Explorer

File   Edit   View   Favorites   Tools   Help

Address http://www.library.uni.edu/instruction/digitalhistory.shtml

Digitized Primary American History Sources

"The Destruction of Tea at Boston Harbor." 1773. Copy of lithograph by Sarony & Major, 1846.

General Sources

This University of Northern Iowa archive offers links to primary source collections on the Web. Scroll down to find links to primary source materials about World War II.

Access this Web site from http://www.myreportlinks.com

▷ Post-World War I Germany

The German government immediately found itself in turmoil after the war. Many Germans believed that their country could have won World War I and felt that the German Army had been betrayed by the German government.[1] The massive payments in reparations strangled the German economy, and the German constitution made things even worse because it encouraged a large number of small political parties, leading to governments that did not last. These problems were compounded by the international economic climate of high inflation.[2] With Germany struggling to make its payments, the French occupied the Ruhr region of Germany in 1923, Germany's chief industrial center. That added to the humiliation of the German people.[3]

▷ The Rise of Adolf Hitler

Out of this political and economic chaos emerged Adolf Hitler. Hitler was the leader of a small radical party in the southern German state of Bavaria. Though an Austrian by birth, he had served in the German Army during World War I as a courier. He only rose to the rank of corporal, but he received several medals for bravery.[4] Hitler's German Workers' party attempted to seize the Bavarian government in November 1923 in a poorly planned revolt. For his involvement, Hitler spent nine months in prison, though his imprisonment was more like a house arrest. While there, he wrote

Mein Kampf ("My Struggle"). It spelled out his belief that history was a record of struggles between races, and the superior Aryan race in Germany ultimately would be victorious.

It was self-evident that the new movement [National Socialism] could hope to achieve the necessary importance and the required strength for this gigantic struggle only if it succeeded from the very first day in arousing in the hearts of its supporters the holy conviction that with it political life was to be given, not

▲ *Adolf Hitler, far left, was a corporal in the German Army in World War I. The harsh treatment of Germany and its people following the First World War helped to sow the seeds of discontent that led to the Second World War.*

to a new election slogan but to a new philosophy of fundamental significance.[5]

A depressed world economy was made worse by the stock market crash in the United States on October 29, 1929, which ushered in the Great Depression and added to the misery and political instability in Germany. Having learned lessons from his failed attempt to seize the Bavarian government, Hitler organized his party. His storm troopers brutally battled Communists in the streets, while he brought the German people a tempting message of hope and a future in which Germany was strong. On January 29, 1933, Germany's president, Paul von Hindenburg, was pressured to appoint Hitler chancellor of Germany. In the next elections, Hitler's party, now known as the National Socialist Workers' party, or Nazi party, passed laws that made Adolf Hitler Germany's dictator.[6]

Germany Rearms

As he took power, Hitler banned all political parties other than the Nazi party. He blamed Jews for Germany's defeat in World War I and began to persecute them. He opened the first concentration camps to house political opponents and other "undesirable" elements of society, which included people who were crippled, had suffered birth defects, or were mentally ill. Other camps were factories of death where millions were killed as part of Hitler's "final solution"

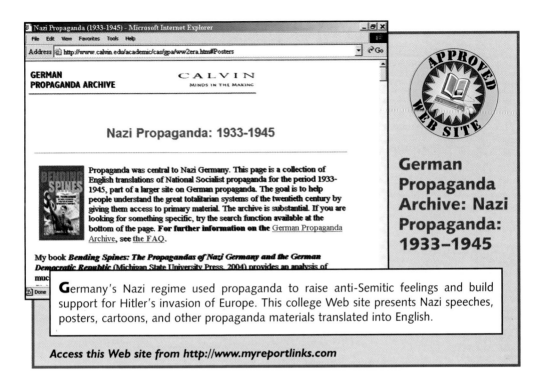

Nazi Propaganda (1933-1945) - Microsoft Internet Explorer

File   Edit   View   Favorites   Tools   Help

Address 🔗 http://www.calvin.edu/academic/cas/gpa/ww2era.htm#Posters   ▾   🔗 Go

GERMAN
PROPAGANDA ARCHIVE

CALVIN
MINDS IN THE MAKING

Nazi Propaganda: 1933-1945

Propaganda was central to Nazi Germany. This page is a collection of English translations of National Socialist propaganda for the period 1933-1945, part of a larger site on German propaganda. The goal is to help people understand the great totalitarian systems of the twentieth century by giving them access to primary material. The archive is substantial. If you are looking for something specific, try the search function available at the bottom of the page. For further information on the German Propaganda Archive, see the FAQ.

My book *Bending Spines: The Propagandas of Nazi Germany and the German Democratic Republic* (Michigan State University Press, 2004) provides an analysis of much

German Propaganda Archive: Nazi Propaganda: 1933–1945

Germany's Nazi regime used propaganda to raise anti-Semitic feelings and build support for Hitler's invasion of Europe. This college Web site presents Nazi speeches, posters, cartoons, and other propaganda materials translated into English.

Access this Web site from http://www.myreportlinks.com

to exterminate the Jews. Hitler also put Germans to work on large public-works programs that rebuilt buildings, stadiums, and highways, including the high-speed roads called autobahns.[7]

Germany also began to rearm itself. According to the Treaty of Versailles, Germany was to have a small army of only around one hundred thousand men, a coastal navy, and no air force.[8] The Rhineland region, an area bordering the Rhine River in western Germany, had been "demilitarized" following the war as a buffer between Germany and France. In violation of the treaty, Hitler expanded the size of the army; created the German Air Force, called the Luftwaffe; and began rebuilding the German Navy.

In 1936, he reoccupied the Rhineland with troops, and France and Great Britain did nothing to stop him. Confident that the former allies of World War I would not act, Hitler sent troops to fight in the Spanish Civil War, which became a training ground for Germany's new equipment and tactics.[9]

The Push for More Territory

Hitler turned his attention to uniting the German-speaking people of Europe. His first move was in his homeland of Austria, where he managed to replace the Austrian chancellor with a Nazi who welcomed German soldiers into Austria. On March 13, 1938, Hitler proclaimed the official union of Germany and Austria.[10]

Hitler then turned to the Sudetenland, a region in Czechoslovakia (now the Czech Republic and Slovakia) that was home to many ethnic Germans. France and Britain opposed the union but could do little because Czechoslovakia could not defend itself in a war against Germany. The leaders of France, Britain, and Germany met at the Munich Conference in September 1938 where they signed an agreement that ceded, or gave, the Sudetenland to Germany but left the rest of Czechoslovakia as a sovereign state. British prime minister Neville Chamberlain claimed that the Munich Agreement guaranteed "Peace in our time."[11] It failed to stop Hitler, and by March 15, 1939, Germany occupied the rest of Czechoslovakia.

Benito Mussolini and Adolf Hitler in Munich, Germany, in June 1940. The Fascist dictator of Italy and the Nazi dictator of Germany had forged a military alliance, known as the Pact of Steel, the year before.

An Alliance With Italy

Benito Mussolini watched Germany's aggressive actions and decided that he wanted to expand his territory as well. Mussolini had set up a Fascist dictatorship in Italy almost a decade before Hitler had come to power. Mussolini's Blackshirts, his Fascist militia that used violence to suppress opponents, served as the early model for the Nazi party.[12] On April 7, 1939, Mussolini attacked the Balkan nation of Albania, a much smaller and poorer country than Italy. To Mussolini, it was a quick and easy victory to claim in rebuilding the Roman Empire.[13] The Albania adventure showed that Mussolini was all bluster, however; the Italian Army's performance was an embarrassment.

The Invasion of Poland

Next on Hitler's list was Poland. Hitler wanted to regain territory lost in the First World War that separated Germany from the state of East Prussia and recover the Baltic port city of Danzig. In August 1939, negotiators for Germany and the Soviet Union signed an agreement not to go to war against each other. The German-Soviet Nonaggression Pact divided Poland between Germany and the Soviet Union. A secret part of the pact, however, divided

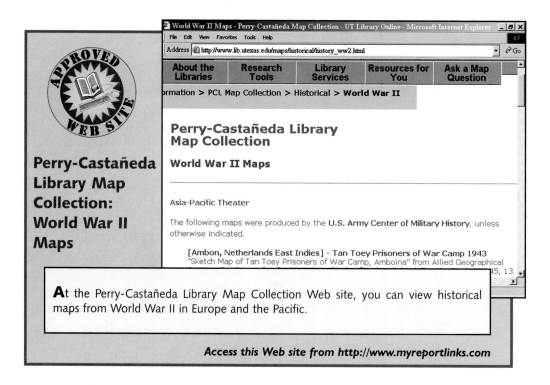

Perry-Castañeda Library Map Collection: World War II Maps

World War II Maps - Perry-Castañeda Map Collection - UT Library Online - Microsoft Internet Explorer

File   Edit   View   Favorites   Tools   Help

Address http://www.lib.utexas.edu/maps/historical/history_ww2.html   Go

| About the Libraries | Research Tools | Library Services | Resources for You | Ask a Map Question |

ormation > PCL Map Collection > Historical > **World War II**

Perry-Castañeda Library Map Collection

World War II Maps

Asia-Pacific Theater

The following maps were produced by the **U.S. Army Center of Military History**, unless otherwise indicated.

[Ambon, Netherlands East Indies] - Tan Toey Prisoners of War Camp 1943
"Sketch Map of Tan Toey Prisoners of War Camp, Amboina" from Allied Geographical

At the Perry-Castañeda Library Map Collection Web site, you can view historical maps from World War II in Europe and the Pacific.

Access this Web site from http://www.myreportlinks.com

up the whole of Eastern Europe into areas controlled by either the Germans or the Soviets. The pact was important to Hitler because an alliance with the Soviet Union meant Germany would only have to face France and Britain in the west—not the Soviet Union in the east. Germany's military planners knew that a war on two fronts would be disastrous.

On September 1, 1939, the German Army invaded Poland. The assault marked the beginning of modern warfare: a new combined-arms strategy of tanks, air strikes, and motorized infantry known as *blitzkrieg,* or "lightning war." The concept was to terrify and disrupt the enemy with air strikes and crash through the enemy's lines rapidly with tanks and motorized infantry to surround the enemy's armies and destroy them quickly. In Poland, the tactic was a success. By September 16, the German Army had surrounded Warsaw, Poland's capital, even though two weeks earlier, Britain and France had declared war on Germany. World War II in Europe had begun.[14]

The Phony War

Poland had no chance. On September 17, the Soviet Union's Red Army poured across Poland's eastern frontiers. The Polish government fled into exile in London on September 19, and Warsaw fell on September 27.

Although Poland's allies, France and Britain, had declared war on Germany, they had no plans to help the Poles. The British had sent about 150,000

This Polish child in Russia, who fled his country after the Nazi invasion, carries bread made from flour that was supplied by the American Red Cross.

men to help France defend the Maginot Line, a series of fortresses linked along France's border with Germany. The Maginot Line was supposed to be impossible to penetrate—it was thought that no German force could get past it. However, there was little fighting along the line, and the war in October became known as the Phony War in American newspapers because of inaction.[15]

The Winter War

In November 1939, Soviet forces attacked Finland in what became known as the Winter War.[16] The small but effective Finnish Army caused the Soviets terrible casualties before the weight of the Soviet forces managed to force a settlement in March 1940. The Soviets lost nearly two hundred thousand men while the Finns lost about twenty-five thousand.[17] The war was resumed in 1941 through 1945 with Finland siding with Germany, but the Finns managed to distance themselves when the German defeat became apparent.

The importance of the Winter War was that the world saw the incompetence of the Soviet military machine. Hitler stored away these perceptions for the future, believing that the Red Army was inept.

Hitler next turned his attention to Norway and Denmark. German industry relied on iron ore from Sweden, and Hitler needed to protect this vital asset by occupying Sweden's neighbors. The Danes surrendered on the day the Germans invaded, April 9, 1940. The Norwegians courageously fought on with some help from the British and French, but by June 8, 1940, Norway surrendered, and British and French troops left Scandinavia. The blitzkrieg had claimed two more victims.[18]

The Low Countries and France

With his eastern flank and iron-ore supplies secure, Hitler turned his attention to France. On May 10,

1940, the Germans began their assault, but not at the Maginot Line. Instead, they attacked Belgium, Holland, and Luxembourg—known as the Low Countries because they lay at or just above sea level—with ruthless efficiency. That same day, Prime Minister Neville Chamberlain of Great Britain resigned and was replaced by Winston Churchill, who directed the British effort for the rest of the war.[19]

Splitting Forces

The French had not anticipated that modern armor could come through the dense Ardennes forest and were taken by surprise when German *panzer*, or armored, divisions emerged. The Allied forces were split, and German armies raced to take advantage.

In fact, the Germans were a little too successful. Unsure whether to race on to Paris or to attack the Maginot Line from behind, the German assault stalled just long enough for the British Army to strike at the Germans. Although unsuccessful, it bought the British time to organize a pocket of defense at the French port of Dunkirk. The British Army was rescued by a makeshift fleet of every vessel the Royal Navy could press into service. From May 26 through August 14, 1940, approximately 558,000 Allied personnel, including over 53,000 French troops, escaped the Germans.[20] Even so, the Germans had nearly sewn up the victory when the Italians leaped into the war on June 10, 1940, on the Axis side, with Germany, Austria, and

These British soldiers were taken as prisoners of war by the Germans at Dunkirk, France, in June 1940, despite valiant efforts by the Royal Navy to rescue them.

their allies. Elsewhere in Europe, all resistance collapsed, and France ordered a general surrender on June 22, 1940. Now Britain stood alone against Hitler and his army of millions.[21]

Bombs Over Britain

During the First World War, Great Britain had endured attacks by air when the Germans used zeppelins, or airships, to bomb London. These attacks hurt civilian morale more than they inflicted serious damage. But with the Second World War, improved technology allowed the Germans to begin a bombing campaign of Great Britain designed to destroy the Royal Air Force (RAF). The German plan was to achieve air superiority first so that Germany could then invade Great Britain by sea. The Germans began planning Operation Sea Lion while they waited for the Luftwaffe to clear the way.

What followed was a duel between air forces that became known as the Battle of Britain. The RAF was at a disadvantage in numbers, but the Luftwaffe was designed for close air support of a ground assault, not long-range strategic bombing. The British also had two of the best fighter planes of the day, the Hawker Hurricane and the Spitfire.[22]

The Luftwaffe first tried to destroy Britain's defenses by attacking British airfields, harbors, and military targets. The Luftwaffe began to overwhelm the RAF's resources even though the Germans suffered serious losses. Then, accidentally, a German

▲ *Children in east London are left homeless after German bombing raids in September 1940. Known as the Blitz, the Nazis' strategic bombing of the United Kingdom and London in particular lasted from September 7, 1940, until May 11, 1941. More than 43,000 lost their lives and more than one million homes were destroyed, but the British people soldiered on.*

plane bombed London.[23] The RAF struck back with a minor raid on Berlin, and Hitler took it as a personal insult. He decided that since the British had bombed Berlin, he would flatten all British cities. He ordered Hermann Göring, the commander of the Luftwaffe, to bomb British cities instead of British military targets. The switch to civilian targets gave the RAF just enough time to regroup and refocus its efforts defending against the German bombers hitting British cities. The continued resistance and mounting losses forced the German military to put off Operation Sea Lion. Finally, the planned invasion

In March 1945, Winston Churchill, third from left, is accompanied by British and American generals as they inspect the antitank defenses known as dragon's teeth that were part of the Siegfried Line. Also known as the West Wall, it was a line of German fortifications on Germany's western border. This image comes from **Churchill and the Great Republic,** a Library of Congress Web site.

of Britain was canceled in October 1940, though the bombing campaign continued until May 1941.[24]

U-boats Prowl the Seas

In addition to the air assault on Britain, the Germans began what was known as the Battle of the Atlantic. Britain, an island nation, needed food and supplies brought in by ship to survive and continue fighting since so many of its people were involved in the war effort. The Germans tried to block those ships from arriving by sending out submarines called U-boats (from the German *Unterseeboot,* "undersea boat"), to sink all shipping around the British Isles. To combat the U-boats, British ships traveled in convoys, or groups, with an escort for protection. The U-boats countered by hunting the convoys with Wolf Packs, organized forces of several U-boats. The British, though, had come up with a new invention, radar, which used radio waves to locate the subs. While U-boats sank more than 2,800 Allied ships and warships, 784 U-boats were lost in the process. Although the U-boats inflicted a lot of damage, by 1943 the Allies had gained the upper hand in the Atlantic.[25]

While the Battle of Britain raged, Prime Minister Winston Churchill made a daring move and shipped reinforcements, or additional troops, to fight the Italians in North Africa. He shipped these men at a time when a German invasion seemed likely any day. The British troops were so successful against the Italians that it quickly became clear that the Germans would have to send support to the Italians in North Africa. The Germans sent General Erwin Rommel and troops called the Afrika Korps. Through aggressive tactics, Rommel managed to push the British back across the desert and into Egypt.

Attack on the Balkans

Hitler made his assault on the Balkan Peninsula on April 6, 1941, with his attack on Yugoslavia. Yugoslavia's defenses quickly crumbled, but the partisan warfare that followed was brutal and used up more German resources. Greece fell soon afterward.

Hitler decided to invade the Greek island of Crete, which the Germans felt would be used by the British as a bomber base to attack Romanian oil fields. The British fought hard to defend the island, but German paratroopers, soldiers who parachuted into battle, managed to capture Crete. With the victory, though, the Germans suffered terrible casualties, and Hitler disbanded his paratrooper corps, deciding that airborne troops were not an effective weapon.[26]

Operation Barbarossa: Germany Invades the Soviet Union

Although Hitler and Stalin had been allies at the war's beginning, Hitler decided as early as 1940 to invade the Soviet Union to expand Germany's borders eastward. That invasion was planned to occur after a British surrender. Even without Britain

General Erwin Rommel (left) earned the nickname Desert Fox for his brilliant military exploits in North Africa, driving the British east to Egypt.

surrendering, however, German forces crossed into the Soviet Union on June 22, 1941. Operation Barbarossa, Germany's code name for its invasion of the Soviet Union, had been delayed five weeks while fighting took place in the Balkans. Those five weeks may ultimately have made the difference in the campaign. Hitler's decision not to send winter supplies to his troops also played a large part.

It took nearly a month before the Red Army started to stiffen. The Soviets used a "scorched earth" strategy that drew the German Army deeper into Soviet Russia, while the retreating Soviets burned and destroyed everything of value to the Germans they could. As a result, the Germans had to rely on long supply lines to feed and equip their troops. By late September 1941, the German Army Group North reached Leningrad, surrounded the city, and began to besiege it. By October, the Germans were within sixty miles of Moscow, the Soviet capital. As the German offensive neared its goal, the brutal winter set in, and the Germans were not prepared for it. Their men did not have enough winter clothing, and there was not enough fuel and effective antifreeze to keep their tanks moving. By November, the German offensive ground to a standstill.

Siege at Stalingrad

By spring, the German Army revived and began attacks in the south against the Soviet Union's oil fields that supplied most of the Red Army. The

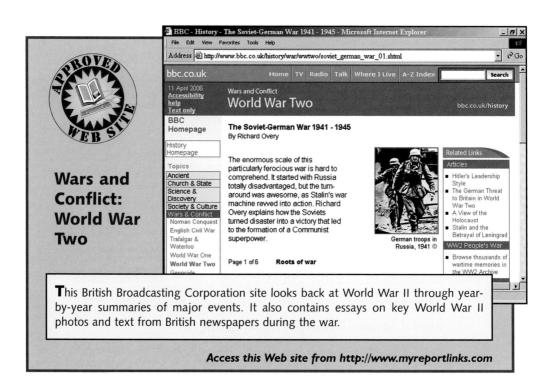

Wars and Conflict: World War Two

BBC - History - The Soviet-German War 1941 - 1945 - Microsoft Internet Explorer

File   Edit   View   Favorites   Tools   Help

Address http://www.bbc.co.uk/history/war/wwtwo/soviet_german_war_01.shtml   Go

bbc.co.uk   Home TV Radio Talk Where I Live A-Z Index   Search

11 April 2006
Accessibility
help
Text only

BBC
Homepage

History
Homepage

Topics
Ancient
Church & State
Science &
Discovery
Society & Culture
Wars & Conflict
Norman Conquest
English Civil War
Trafalgar &
Waterloo
World War One
World War Two
Genocide

Wars and Conflict
World War Two   bbc.co.uk/history

The Soviet-German War 1941 - 1945
By Richard Overy

The enormous scale of this particularly ferocious war is hard to comprehend. It started with Russia totally disadvantaged, but the turn-around was awesome, as Stalin's war machine revved into action. Richard Overy explains how the Soviets turned disaster into a victory that led to the formation of a Communist superpower.

German troops in Russia, 1941 ©

Page 1 of 6   **Roots of war**

Related Links

Articles

- Hitler's Leadership Style
- The German Threat to Britain in World War Two
- A View of the Holocaust
- Stalin and the Betrayal of Leningrad

WW2 People's War

- Browse thousands of wartime memories in the WW2 Archive

This British Broadcasting Corporation site looks back at World War II through year-by-year summaries of major events. It also contains essays on key World War II photos and text from British newspapers during the war.

Access this Web site from http://www.myreportlinks.com

Red Army decided to take a stand at the southern Russian city of Stalingrad. The Soviets lured a major German force into Stalingrad and then used a military maneuver known as a pincer movement to surround the Germans in the city. The pincer attack surprised Hitler, who had underestimated the Soviet forces in the area, and he ordered his commander of the German forces in Stalingrad to defend the city. Luftwaffe commander Hermann Göring declared that he could keep the city supplied, though this claim was completely unrealistic.[27]

Cut off, starving, and freezing to death, the German forces at Stalingrad surrendered on February 2, 1943. In the battle, the Germans lost more than 250,000 men, while the Soviets lost more than 500,000.[28] The Stalingrad trap had worn down the Germans. They could not replace the men and equipment they had lost, while the Soviets could still draw on reinforcements. The Soviet Union had also been saved by supplies from the United States transferred through the Lend-Lease Act passed by the U.S. Congress in 1941, before the United States entered the war. In lend-lease, food and machinery were given to nations whose defense was considered vital to United States' interests.

The Raid at Dieppe

Unable to mount a major invasion of the continent by themselves, the British military and Churchill wanted to strike back at the Germans any way they could to keep up morale. The British created commando units to strike the coasts. Commandos were the first modern Special Forces units. Initial commando raids on small targets were successful and convinced the British to use them on a larger scale. The plan the Allied command devised called for the commandos to land with artillery and tanks near the French port of Dieppe, hold it for twelve hours, capture the German headquarters to get intelligence information, and then escape back to the ships.

The raid on Dieppe was botched from the start. The Allies lost the critical element of any successful commando raid—surprise—when the fleet was discovered in the English Channel by German forces.

▲ *Members of the Red Army in 1941. The Soviet forces would have suffered even more during the Second World War if the United States had not provided them with food and other aid.*

The commandos landed on August 19, 1942, and met a hail of German fire from well-fortified positions. The commandos made no progress and finally retreated back to their ships. Still, the Allies had learned vital lessons in amphibious warfare, operations in which both land and naval forces travel by sea to land on a hostile shore.[29]

▷ Montgomery Versus Rommel

In North Africa, the war continued to see-saw back and forth across the desert. Rommel, heavily outnumbered, attacked but was limited by his stretching supply lines. The British counterattacked and pushed Rommel back. After a major victory over the British at Tobruk, a port city in northeastern Libya, Rommel chose to pursue the fleeing British into Egypt. The Allies managed to hold the Afrika Korps at the First Battle of El Alamein in June 1942.

Though the British had stopped Rommel, Churchill appointed General Bernard Montgomery as the commander of the British Eighth Army in Africa. Desperate to reach the Nile River, Rommel decided to gamble on another attack, but on October 23, 1942, Montgomery attacked at El Alamein. Rommel escaped westward but not before abandoning most of his Italian allies, who had no transportation. Within three months after the Second Battle of El Alamein, Montgomery had captured all of neighboring Libya and was poised to seize Tunisia.[30]

Troops led by British general Bernard Law Montgomery, with reinforcements from the United States, struck back at Rommel's Afrika Korps in 1942 and pushed the Germans back, capturing Libya. By May 1943, the last German troops in North Africa had surrendered to the Allies.

Montgomery's troops were reinforced by the first American troops to fight in the European theater. Led by Generals Dwight Eisenhower and George S. Patton, the Americans landed in Algeria on November 8, 1942, as part of Operation Torch.[31] American soldiers experienced their first action against Rommel in February 1943 at Kasserine Pass, a gap in the Atlas Mountains in Tunisia. Although they were not victorious there, they learned from the campaign. By May 13, 1943, the last German troops in Africa surrendered. The African war was over.[32]

▷ Other Action in 1943

On the eastern front against the Soviets, the Germans launched a massive armored assault on the Soviet forces at Kursk, in southwestern Russia, early in July 1943. The Soviets anticipated the attack and planned complex defenses to wear down the German Army. After suffering heavy casualties and losing many tanks, the Germans were slowed and then faced a pounding counterattack from Soviet forces. The Battle of Kursk represented Germany's last offensive on the eastern front. The Soviets then began their push toward Berlin.[33]

Hitler and his generals faced other problems. On July 10, British and American forces invaded Sicily. On July 25, Hitler's ally, Benito Mussolini, was overthrown. That meant that the German military, its resources already stretched thin, had to remove troops from the eastern front and invade Italy to keep it from changing sides and to protect Germany's southern borders.[34]

The Soviets fought to relieve the siege of Leningrad, which they finally achieved on January 27, 1944. The city had survived more than two years of war. Throughout the spring of 1944, the Soviets slowly but continuously pushed the Germans back westward. By summer, the Soviet assault became easier because the German Army had to withdraw troops to defend Germany from an attack from the west.

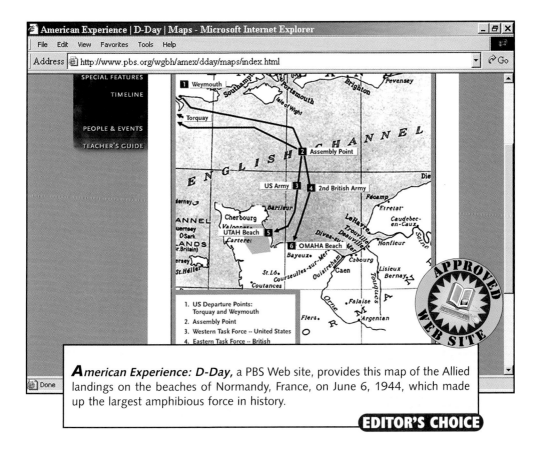

American Experience: D-Day, a PBS Web site, provides this map of the Allied landings on the beaches of Normandy, France, on June 6, 1944, which made up the largest amphibious force in history.

EDITOR'S CHOICE

The D-Day Invasion

The Germans needed to pull troops west because on June 6, 1944, British and American armies launched Operation Overlord, the invasion of Western Europe, also known as D-Day. Planned by General Dwight D. Eisenhower, who had been appointed Supreme Commander of the Allied Expeditionary Force in Europe, the D-Day invasion was the largest amphibious assault in history, with landings on the beaches of Normandy in northwestern France. The Allied soldiers who made it onto the beaches of France then had to break through the Atlantic

http://www.dwightdeisenhower.com/ddayphotos/65x325x3.jpg - Microsoft Internet Explorer

File Edit View Favorites Tools Help

Address http://www.dwightdeisenhower.com/ddayphotos/65x325x3.jpg

General Dwight D. Eisenhower, the Supreme Commander of the Allied Expeditionary Force in Europe and the architect of Operation Overlord, speaks to American paratroopers on June 5, the day before the Normandy invasion. The photograph and other archival resources can be found on the **Dwight D. Eisenhower Presidential Library: D-Day** Web site.

Wall, a line of German fortifications along the coasts of France and Belgium designed to stop just such an invasion.

The location of the invasion, however, came as a surprise to the German military because Allied intelligence had convinced the Germans that the Allies would land near Calais. Calais, a shorter distance across the English Channel, would have made an easier landing position. The Germans, believing at first that the Normandy landings were a diversion, held back critical reinforcements for the Allied attack on Calais that never came.[35]

Paris Is Liberated

The Allies still faced stiff resistance, caught up for six weeks in heavy fighting at the village of Caen and a slow advance to Cherbourg. Ferocious German counterattacks failed largely because the Germans lacked supplies: American and British bombing of German industrial centers was taking a heavy toll. Allied air superiority also hindered Germany's efforts to supply its troops at the front. By late July, the Allied forces had managed to break out. On August 25, 1944, Allied troops liberated Paris from German control. Disorganization caused by the rapid Allied advance and personal disagreements between generals of the various Allied countries over strategy slowed Allied momentum, however.[36]

To regain lost momentum, the Allies planned and executed Operation Market Garden in September

1944. The operation consisted of an airborne attack, or Market phase, seizing waterways, bridges, and railroad. This came in advance of the Garden phase, a ground maneuver in which the British Second Army was to reach the Dutch city of Arnhem. The attack, from September 17 through the 26, failed because the Germans counterattacked before the British tanks reached Arnhem. Operation Market Garden did capture some important territory to launch future offensives, however. By October, Allied forces had pushed into Germany itself.

▶ The Battle of the Bulge

On December 16, 1944, Hitler staged one last counterattack to push the Allies back out of Western Europe with blitzkrieg tactics, though he lacked air support. It would also use up his last armored reserve units. This final attack by the German Army was known as the Battle of the Bulge because it punched a salient, or bulge, in the Allied line. It was fought under the most difficult conditions, with snow and subfreezing temperatures in the Ardennes, a wooded plateau. The Germans pushed into Belgium and surrounded an American force at Bastogne. When asked by the Germans to surrender, General Anthony McAuliffe, the American commander, replied, "Nuts!"[37] The American forces fought on. The Germans quickly lost initiative, and American counterattacks led by General George

American Experience | Battle of the Bulge | Gallery - Microsoft Internet Explorer

File   Edit   View   Favorites   Tools   Help

Address http://www.pbs.org/wgbh/amex/bulge/gallery/gal_bulge_08.html

AMERICAN EXPERIENCE

BATTLE OF
THE BULGE

THE FILM & MORE
SPECIAL FEATURES
TIMELINE
GALLERY
PEOPLE & EVENTS
TEACHER'S GUIDE

Gallery: Battle of the Bulge   ◀ 8 of 12 ▶

NATIONAL ARCHIVES

American Experience: Battle of the Bulge, a PBS Web site, offers archival images and primary source documents of the prolonged final major battle of the war in Europe, fought under terribly harsh conditions as this photo shows.

Patton relieved Bastogne. By February 1945, the Allies were crossing the Rhine River.

The End of War in Europe

In August, Soviet troops pushed into Romania and the Balkans. This cost the Germans their all-important oil source. It virtually grounded the Luftwaffe and made the German Army, once a fast and highly maneuverable force, much slower than the Allied forces. The Red Army continued to push closer to Germany's borders. By early 1945, Soviet forces had entered Germany, and on April 19, Soviet tanks occupied

▲ *The United States Army coming from the west and the Soviet Army coming from the east finally made contact with each other on April 25, 1945. Second Lieutenant William Robertson (left), an American, greets Lieutenant Alexander Sylvashko, a Russian, near Torgau, Germany, on that historic day.*

Berlin's outskirts. Allied and Soviet troops made contact at Torgau on April 25, 1945, splitting Germany.[38] On April 30, the Soviets controlled the German capital, and Adolf Hitler committed suicide in a bunker. On May 1, 1945, the German military asked the Soviets for an armistice, an end to the fighting. Berlin surrendered, though fighting continued.

On May 7, 1945, in Reims, France, Germany surrendered unconditionally, with the fighting to cease on 11:01 P.M. the following day. The Soviets insisted on a separate signing in Berlin on May 9. After six brutal years, the war in Europe was over.[39]

A BRIEF HISTORY OF THE WAR IN THE PACIFIC

While the attack on Pearl Harbor brought the United States into World War II, the war in the Pacific had been raging for several years. The Japanese invaded China on July 7, 1937, conquering most of the coastal areas and major cities.

The roots of the war in the Pacific go back even further than those in Europe. In 1853, the American fleet opened up the isolated feudal society of Japan, and the leaders of Japan began to modernize their country.[1] Japan had seen European countries make colonies of its Asian neighbors and wanted to avoid the same fate. Japan adopted western technology and industry and built a powerful army and navy. But Japan did not have enough materials to build up these forces, so it had to import them.

▷ The Russo-Japanese War and World War I

The Japanese protected what they considered areas vital to their national interest. In 1904, they went to war with Russia to secure the critical city of Port Arthur, which Russia had earlier leased from China. Japan then invaded Korea and Manchuria. The Japanese defeated the Russians, the first time an

▲ Japanese soldiers on the lookout for an attack from Russian cavalry during the Russo-Japanese War, 1906. Japan's victory over Russia gave the small island nation a prestige it had not experienced before.

Asian country had been victorious over a western one on the battlefield. The victory brought prestige to the Japanese military. The Japanese also joined the Allied powers in World War I and seized German possessions in the Pacific. Japan's status had risen, but it remained a junior partner to the United States and Great Britain, which upset some Japanese leaders.[2]

During the 1920s and 1930s, a series of natural disasters, the economic woes of the Great Depression, and new trade restrictions damaged the Japanese economy. Militant nationalists gained momentum in Japan, much as they had in Italy and Germany.

Japan Invades China

Chinese and Japanese armies skirmished through the 1930s. The Japanese held Manchuria, a Chinese province. Japan decided to expand its holdings in China to secure needed raw materials, so in the summer of 1937, Japan invaded China.[3] The Japanese military was successful, but it had achieved success by committing atrocities against Chinese soldiers and civilians. The Chinese fought back by using guerrilla tactics, but soon Japan controlled most of the Chinese coast, while the Chinese held on to mountainous inland territories.

Japanese leaders realized that to conquer China, they would need fuel resources to keep the military running. Japan had no such resources, and western countries would not supply Japan. The Japanese decided to erase European colonial powers from East Asia by setting up the Greater East Asia Co-prosperity Sphere. In effect, it established Japan as an empire to give the Japanese access to needed raw materials.[4]

An Alliance With Germany

When Germany invaded Poland in 1939, Japan became involved because it had signed treaties of alliance with the Germans. British, French, and Dutch forces were engaged in Europe, giving the Japanese a chance to seize European colonies in Asia without much of a fight. It also gave the Japanese a chance to cut off Chinese supply routes through Southeast Asia. The war in Europe also forced America to prepare for war. While the Royal Navy had to focus on the threat in the Atlantic, the U.S. Navy could use its powerful fleet to stop Japan.

Attack on Pearl Harbor

Expecting the Japanese to strike south, the United States imposed a trade embargo on Japan, and on August 1, 1941, froze all Japanese assets in America. Both events were devastating to the Japanese economy, and Japan faced the threat of running out of oil by the middle of 1944 if not earlier.[5] The Japanese government would not pull its troops out of

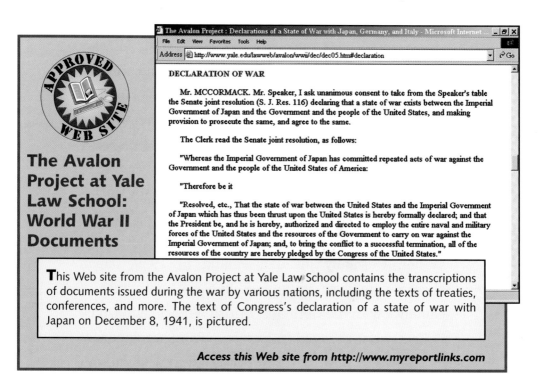

The Avalon Project at Yale Law School: World War II Documents

DECLARATION OF WAR

Mr. MCCORMACK. Mr. Speaker, I ask unanimous consent to take from the Speaker's table the Senate joint resolution (S. J. Res. 116) declaring that a state of war exists between the Imperial Government of Japan and the Government and the people of the United States, and making provision to prosecute the same, and agree to the same.

The Clerk read the Senate joint resolution, as follows:

"Whereas the Imperial Government of Japan has committed repeated acts of war against the Government and the people of the United States of America:

"Therefore be it

"Resolved, etc., That the state of war between the United States and the Imperial Government of Japan which has thus been thrust upon the United States is hereby formally declared; and that the President be, and he is hereby, authorized and directed to employ the entire naval and military forces of the United States and the resources of the Government to carry on war against the Imperial Government of Japan; and, to bring the conflict to a successful termination, all of the resources of the country are hereby pledged by the Congress of the United States."

This Web site from the Avalon Project at Yale Law School contains the transcriptions of documents issued during the war by various nations, including the texts of treaties, conferences, and more. The text of Congress's declaration of a state of war with Japan on December 8, 1941, is pictured.

Access this Web site from http://www.myreportlinks.com

already-occupied territories, so the Japanese military had to strike south. In doing so, Japan would have to seize the Philippines, a United States possession. That action would certainly bring the United States into the war with its large battle fleet stationed at Pearl Harbor in Hawaii. On December 7, 1941, air strikes from Japanese aircraft carriers attacked Pearl Harbor to destroy the U.S. fleet.

At the same time as it attacked Pearl Harbor, Japan launched an attack on Malaya, Hong Kong, Guam, the Philippines, and Wake Island. The war in the Pacific theater was under way. By February, the Japanese had taken Singapore, the largest British base in East Asia, which was a shattering blow to British prestige and morale. They captured the Dutch East Indies in March. The Japanese had fought the Americans through Bataan in the Philippines and finally accepted the American sur-render of the Philippine Islands at Corregidor on May 6, 1942. By May 20, the Japanese had run the British out of Burma and into India.

These early successes left the Japanese with a deci-sion: Since their military objectives had been met so quickly, the Japanese command was unsure whether to continue its assaults in Australia or Hawaii.[6]

▷ Bombing Raids and Carrier Clashes

The U.S. Navy struck at the Japanese as best it could, with air raids against the Gilbert and Marshall islands. On April 18, 1942, Colonel James

Doolittle led a raid on Tokyo with sixteen B-25 bombers. Although Doolittle's raid did little actual damage, it convinced Japanese planners that they had to strike east against Midway Island.[7]

Meanwhile, the Japanese military tried to seize Port Moresby, in New Guinea. The U.S. Navy learned of this attack and moved to intercept the Japanese fleet. The first battle between carriers was fought at the Battle of the Coral Sea on May 7 and 8, 1942, where the U.S. carriers *Lexington* and *Yorktown* managed to sink the Japanese carrier *Shoho* and damage the *Shokaku*. The *Lexington* was also lost,

Photographs - Microsoft Internet Explorer

File   Edit   View   Favorites   Tools   Help

Address http://archives.nmsu.edu/exhibits/thomas/lgphotos.html#c

Gerald W. Thomas in World War II: An Exhibition is a university Web site offering images and letters of a Navy pilot who flew missions in both the Atlantic and Pacific theaters of war. This image shows a landing signal officer aboard a carrier waving a pilot in at a right turn.

however, and the *Yorktown* suffered serious damage.[8] The Japanese were forced to call off their attack on Port Moresby. The battle gave the Allies a chance to build up their defenses in New Guinea and slow the Japanese advance.

The Turning Point: Midway

The turning point came at the Battle of Midway. The Japanese intended to capture Midway Island to prevent further attacks on Japan's mainland. They sent a large fleet to take the position, but what they did not know was that the Americans had broken some of their secret communications codes. Not expecting the U.S. Navy to be in the area, the Japanese fleet was surprised on June 4, 1942, by planes from the U.S. carriers *Enterprise* and *Hornet* and a quickly repaired *Yorktown*. The Japanese lost all four of their aircraft carriers, while the U.S. Navy only lost the *Yorktown*. The balance of naval power had shifted in the Pacific.[9]

The Japanese and Allies engaged in heavy fighting at Guadalcanal and New Guinea. The Japanese won a hard-fought victory at the Battle of Savo Island and then slowly but steadily lost ground until Japanese forces were pushed out of the Solomon Island chain early in 1944.

Submarine Warfare

The U.S. Navy's submarine campaign against the Japanese was more successful. An island nation,

Japan relied on supplies shipped in from other places to keep its industry functioning and its people fed. The Americans instituted a submarine blockade of Japan. Faulty torpedoes issued by the U.S. Navy slowed the campaign's progress, but as soon as the torpedo problems were worked out, the effects were felt almost immediately. Throughout the war, the American submarine fleet sank more than 60 percent of all Japanese ships and slowly strangled Japan's war effort. By the end of 1944, Japan faced massive food and fuel shortages.[10] While Germany's U-boats had failed against Britain, the American submarine forces were much more successful in helping to defeat the Japanese.

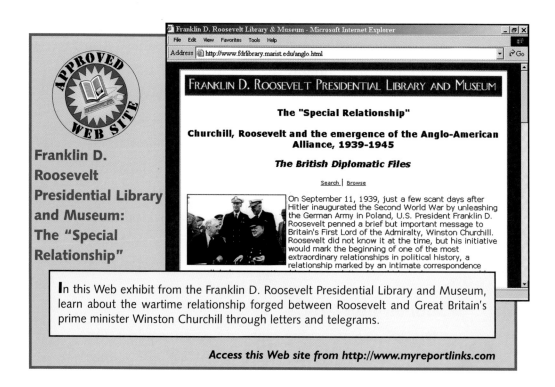

Franklin D. Roosevelt Presidential Library and Museum: The "Special Relationship"

FRANKLIN D. ROOSEVELT PRESIDENTIAL LIBRARY AND MUSEUM

The "Special Relationship"

Churchill, Roosevelt and the emergence of the Anglo-American Alliance, 1939-1945

The British Diplomatic Files

Search | Browse

On September 11, 1939, just a few scant days after Hitler inaugurated the Second World War by unleashing the German Army in Poland, U.S. President Franklin D. Roosevelt penned a brief but important message to Britain's First Lord of the Admiralty, Winston Churchill. Roosevelt did not know it at the time, but his initiative would mark the beginning of one of the most extraordinary relationships in political history, a relationship marked by an intimate correspondence

In this Web exhibit from the Franklin D. Roosevelt Presidential Library and Museum, learn about the wartime relationship forged between Roosevelt and Great Britain's prime minister Winston Churchill through letters and telegrams.

Access this Web site from http://www.myreportlinks.com

These U.S. Marines were part of the bitter fight at Tarawa, in the Gilbert Islands, November 1943. The Gilbert Islands, in the western Pacific, are now part of Kiribati, a nation made up of three island chains.

The Americans Advance on Japan

As the fighting in the southwest Pacific wound down, American military planners came up with a course of action to advance on the Japanese. General Douglas MacArthur wanted to stage an assault on New Guinea to retake the Philippines, while Admiral Chester Nimitz wanted to move through the central Pacific. By late 1943, the U.S. Navy had rebuilt its fleet enough to pursue that plan. Its first target was Tarawa in the Gilbert Islands. Tarawa was a bitter fight, but the rest of the Gilbert Islands fell relatively easily. The U.S. Marines, aided by the Navy, captured the Marshall Islands, and by February, were staging raids on the Japanese naval station at Truk, in the Caroline Islands.[11]

MacArthur Advances

Meanwhile, General MacArthur pushed his forces ahead. They bypassed the large Japanese garrison at Rabaul and took lightly defended garrisons to the north and west, in a move known as island hopping. This isolated the Rabaul garrison, making it useless.

The U.S. Navy advanced on the Mariana Islands, especially Saipan, Guam, and Tinian, which were within bombing range of Japan. The Japanese responded with a massive fleet and every airplane they could send, but fuel shortages meant Japan's pilots lacked training, and Japan had lost many of its best pilots and planes already. Its outdated aircraft were easy targets for the now better-trained and better-equipped American fighter pilots. The resulting battle was known as the Marianas Turkey Shoot because the Japanese lost more than four hundred planes to the Americans' thirty.[12] Three of the eight Japanese carriers in the battle were sunk, two by submarines. The Marines fought a savage battle against the Japanese defenders, and many Japanese fighters and civilians chose suicide rather than surrender to the Americans. Saipan fell to the Allies on July 9, 1944.

The British, meanwhile, began to make headway against the Japanese in Burma. After several failed advances in 1942 and 1943, the British began to score small successes with Special Forces units called Chindits who worked behind the Japanese lines. While the damage inflicted on the Japanese was not great, it provided a morale boost for the Allies. In March 1944, the Japanese staged a major offensive against Imphal and Kohima in India, surrounding the British forces, but the Japanese were also low on supplies and ammunition and suffering heavy casualties. Japan was forced to call off the offensive.[13] The way was cleared for a British advance once the monsoon, or rainy, season had passed.

Fighting in China

China remained a problem for Japan. The Nationalist Chinese forces under Jiang Jie-shi, better known as Chiang Kai-shek, continued to resist the Japanese, but the Chinese Communist party's guerrilla campaign under Mao Zedong was even more effective. Chiang

General Chiang Kai-shek became the leader of the Republic of China in 1928. He led China in its second war with Japan, but was ultimately defeated by the Chinese Communists in China's civil war, and his Nationalist government fled to the island of Taiwan.

Kai-shek had started conserving his Nationalist Army for the civil war with the Chinese Communists that he felt was sure to follow when Japan lost the war. While not a major campaign, the war in China involved a million Japanese soldiers and drained Japan's resources, further weakening Japan's war effort.

The Final Campaigns

Late in the summer of 1944, the Japanese Empire still seemed strong, but the Japanese Navy was a shell of its former self, losing many ships and most of its experienced pilots. The Japanese Army seemed incapable of stopping American advances in the southwest Pacific. The American submarine offensive was choking the Japanese economy, and Japan's industries and people suffered as a result.

Early in September, carrier strikes confirmed that strong Japanese garrisons at Yap and Talaud, on nearby islands, and Sarangani, an island in the Philippines, could be avoided and that a landing in the Philippines was possible. To prevent the Allied landing in the Philippines, the Japanese sent what was left of their fleet to Leyte Gulf. The Battle of Leyte Gulf, which began on October 23, 1944, proved to be one of the largest and most decisive naval battles in history. Japan lost four carriers, three battleships, nine cruisers, and ten destroyers as well as more than five hundred aircraft.[14] The defeat destroyed the Japanese Navy, and Japan lost control of the Philippines after weeks of desperate fighting. By the end of June 1945, the Philippines were firmly in American hands.

British forces began their push in Burma in December 1944, crossing the Chindwin River and taking Rangoon, the capital, on May 3, 1945. They were in place to begin an invasion of Malaya late in the summer to clear it of Japanese troops.[15]

Iwo Jima and Okinawa

In March 1945, American forces seized Iwo Jima, the largest of the Volcano Islands and the site of a Japanese air base. By capturing it, Allied bombers could launch raids on Japan with fighter escorts to protect them—and deprive Japan of a two-hour

▲ *When the Philippines fell to the Japanese in 1942, General Douglas MacArthur just barely escaped, and he pledged to return. His triumphant reentry is recorded in this image as he and his officers wade ashore at Leyte on October 20, 1944.*

▲ *U.S. Marines of the Fourth Division shell concealed Japanese positions on the black sand beaches of the small volcanic island of Iwo Jima, February 1945. It took a month of brutal fighting before the island was captured by American forces.*

warning of Allied raids since planes had to fly over Iwo Jima to reach the Japanese mainland.

The fighting on Iwo Jima was the bloodiest in the Pacific to that time. In their desperation, the Japanese had turned the entire island into a fortress of cave complexes. It took a month of heavy fighting to finally clear the island of its defenders. As bloody as Iwo Jima was, the fighting at Okinawa, in Japan's Ryuku Islands, was even worse. The Japanese defended the island with suicide attacks by pilots who flew their planes loaded with bombs into American ships. These pilots were known as *kamikazes,* or "divine wind," after a storm that had saved Japan from a medieval Mongol invasion. Kamikaze attacks sank thirty-six American ships and damaged almost four hundred.[16]

The battles of Iwo Jima and Okinawa disturbed American military planners who were trying to draw up plans for the invasion of Japan. The U.S. Marines suffered huge casualties at the hands of the kamikazes. The Americans had begun a bombing campaign that flattened several Japanese cities, including Tokyo, Japan's capital, but the Allied planners wanted to avoid the casualties on both sides that it feared would result from an invasion of Japan.

November 1, 1945, was the date of the planned invasion, but American and British commands decided to end the war before that. This was to avoid casualties and also to avoid significant Soviet participation. On July 26, 1945, the Americans demanded that the Japanese surrender. The Japanese refused on July 28, 1945.[17]

Hiroshima and Nagasaki

On August 6, 1945, a single B-29 bomber dropped an atomic bomb, a weapon never before used in war, on the Japanese city of Hiroshima, a port city on the island of Honshu. In a flash, the city disappeared, the first city to suffer the attack of an atomic weapon. It is estimated that the blast killed sixty-six thousand people and severely injured sixty-nine thousand. Despite the devastation, Japan refused to surrender, hoping it could leverage the Soviets

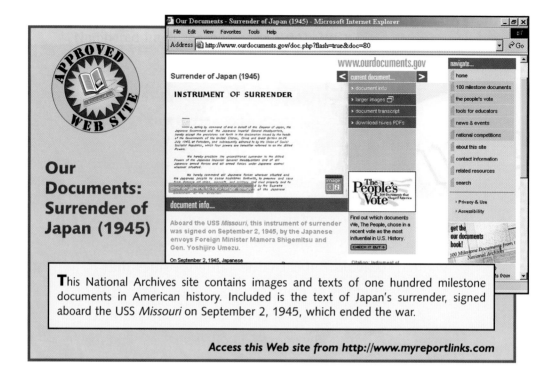

Our Documents: Surrender of Japan (1945)

This National Archives site contains images and texts of one hundred milestone documents in American history. Included is the text of Japan's surrender, signed aboard the USS *Missouri* on September 2, 1945, which ended the war.

Access this Web site from http://www.myreportlinks.com

against the Americans for better surrender terms. The Soviets, however, declared war on Japan, and the Red Army invaded Manchuria on August 8.

On August 9, the Americans dropped a second atomic bomb, this time on Nagasaki, a port city on Kyushu. Japan continued two more weeks of fighting with Soviet forces, who were trying to secure as much land as possible, but on August 14, 1945, Japan accepted the surrender terms of the Allies. At noon on August 15, 1945, World War II ended in the Pacific theater of operations. The formal surrender ending World War II was signed on September 2, 1945, on the deck of the USS *Missouri*, anchored in Tokyo Harbor.[18]

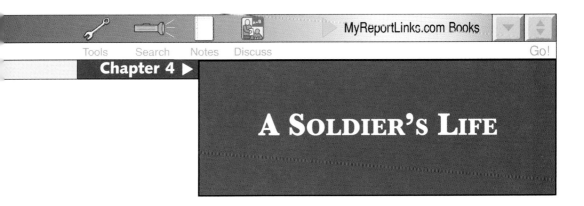
Chapter 4 ▶

A SOLDIER'S LIFE

Even in a war as deadly as World War II, soldiers were not constantly in combat. Much of their time was spent adapting to their daily routines as well as to strange places and new and unusual circumstances.

Chow Time

It is said that an army travels on its stomach, and the difficulties of feeding armies of millions of men during the Second World War were enormous. James Baross of the Army Air Corps stationed in New Guinea recalls how he and some fellow soldiers were able to vary their diet.

> . . . as we approached the mess tent, men there with cleavers hacked off the tops of cans of salmon, which they then inverted and shook, and shook, and shook over our mess kits until, with a sucking, wet, schlushy sound the contents of the can would come sliding out, at which time another man would cover the salmon with a large chunk of bread.
>
> At one place in the camp was a large . . . tent, guarded by two GIs during the day and the night. We became fascinated by what the tent might contain, checked a bit, and . . . found that it contained cases,

▲ *American soldiers of the 347th Infantry Regiment line up for food during their march to La Roche, Belgium, January 13, 1945, during the Battle of the Bulge, which claimed more than 75,000 American casualties.*

cases, and cases stacked to the top of prepared fruits from Tasmania.

Baross and his buddies had some of their group distract the soldiers guarding the tent while a few of them entered the tent from behind and carried out case after case of peaches, apricots, pears, and apples. From that night, Baross and his friends "did not stand in a wavering line with . . . mess kits in hand waiting for . . . dinner of canned salmon." As Baross admitted after the war, "I, to this day, cannot eat canned apricots without thinking fondly of my dinners at Port Moresby."[1]

Not all soldiers had such fond memories of the food they were served during the war. Some thought it might be more useful as a secret weapon. In his memoirs, Malcolm Stilson, who served in the Army Air Corps, recalls one such comment.

While in the mess hall one day, I found some graffiti on the wall that helped to while away the time while standing in line. Some wit wrote it while he was standing in line waiting for the delicious meal ahead. "Food will win the war, but how are we going to get the enemy to eat here?"[2]

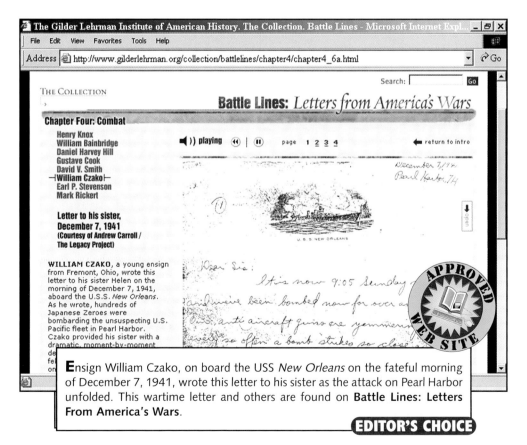

The Gilder Lehrman Institute of American History. The Collection. Battle Lines - Microsoft Internet Expl...

File   Edit   View   Favorites   Tools   Help

Address http://www.gilderlehrman.org/collection/battlelines/chapter4/chapter4_6a.html

Search:

THE COLLECTION

Battle Lines: *Letters from America's Wars*

Chapter Four: Combat

Henry Knox
William Bainbridge
Daniel Harvey Hill
Gustave Cook
David V. Smith
—|William Czako|—
Earl P. Stevenson
Mark Rickert

**Letter to his sister,
December 7, 1941**
(Courtesy of Andrew Carroll /
The Legacy Project)

WILLIAM CZAKO, a young ensign from Fremont, Ohio, wrote this letter to his sister Helen on the morning of December 7, 1941, aboard the U.S.S. *New Orleans*. As he wrote, hundreds of Japanese Zeroes were bombarding the unsuspecting U.S. Pacific fleet in Pearl Harbor. Czako provided his sister with a dramatic, moment-by-moment de...

playing   page 1 2 3 4   return to intro

Ensign William Czako, on board the USS *New Orleans* on the fateful morning of December 7, 1941, wrote this letter to his sister as the attack on Pearl Harbor unfolded. This wartime letter and others are found on **Battle Lines: Letters From America's Wars**.

EDITOR'S CHOICE

Stilson had fonder memories of mail call. In the midst of war, receiving letters from home helped boost a soldier's morale tremendously.

The man with the mail throws up his arms to protect himself, and then he is suddenly obscured by a group of shouting, gesticulating creatures who bear little resemblance to soldiers. Suddenly someone with a loud voice shouts, "At ease!" and there is a sudden hush in the barracks. Tense excitement grips everyone as the names of the lucky mail receivers are shouted out. The men fortunate enough to have letters return to their bunks with happy faces and singing hearts, while the other unfortunates droop down the aisle, hopes shattered, morale broken, with nothing to live for. I know it ruined my morale not to receive mail for a while.[3]

▶ Lightening the Mood

Soldiers have always used humor to lighten the stress of warfare. The following "instructions" were intended to help them adjust to civilian society, telling them how they should act when they returned home on leave:

The United States is composed of land. Bisecting the center is the Mississippi River. Everything east of the river is known as New York, while everything west is simply called Texas. There are a couple of other states, but they are not important. . . . Food is generally plentiful [and in] many restaurants you will see an item called "steak" on the menu. This dish is to be eaten with knife and fork. Steak has a meaty taste and isn't too revolting after one gets used to it. Of course, it doesn't come up to the luscious delectability of our own Bully Beef. . . .[4]

"Bully Beef" is the beef equivalent to spam—a canned meat. Most soldiers were in agreement: They hated it.

All mail sent by servicemen was censored by the military, which often frustrated loved ones back home trying to learn about their soldier's welfare. A soldier's peculiar sense of humor could be almost as frustrating to friends and loved ones. Private First Class William Lee Kyzer penned these few lines, which must have made his readers wonder just what was going on.

Dear Dad & Carmilita

I'm OK, days fly by here in Well maybe it can be all again soon. I'm praying for it. Write soon Nothing like getting a letter from home. Here on

Love
Bill
P.S. They may censor this letter[5]

In fact "they," the military censors, did not change his words. PFC Kyzer hated writing letters, so he just wrote a few lines at the top and bottom of the page and let the U.S. Army censors take the blame for the choppy wording.

 *The weariness of war is echoed from one generation to the next. Sergeant Norwood Dorman of North Carolina, an American soldier in Brolo, Sicily, in 1943, takes a rest on the steps of a memorial to Italian soldiers who fought in World War I.*

The military did try to give the troops an escape from the war and the boredom that went with it, if only for a little while. James Baross of the Army Air Corps remembers a "night out" at the movies:

Showings were on a screen stretched between two palm trees and we sat on the ground. . . . unless it was raining, which it did about half the time.

When it rained, we sat on our helmets and draped our ponchos over our heads with the hole, through which the head was supposed to go, right in front of our eyes. It made for dry watching of the movie.

The same movie would be shown for as long as we had it, usually a couple of weeks. Boredom caused many of us to attend night after night until we could narrate the actors' lines along with them.[6]

UNDER FIRE

A soldier's most terrifying experience during combat comes when he is under enemy fire. Sergeant Alvin Josephy, Jr., a Marine Corps correspondent, described the conditions during a ferocious Japanese attack on the island of Guam.

> The Marines awoke with a start. Along the ridge, wet, groggy men bolted to their feet and grabbed their weapons. Grenades exploded like a crashing curtain against the onrushing Japs. A man on the telephone yelled for uninterrupted flares, and flickering lights began to hang in the air like giant overhead fires.
>
> All along the line the enemy attack was on. Red tracer bullets flashed through the blackness. Japanese orange signal flares and American white illumination shells lit up the night like the Fourth of July, silhouetting the running forms of the enemy. On the right and the left the attack was stopped cold. As fast as the Japs came, they were mowed down by automatic rifles and machine guns.[1]

▶ Remembering Normandy

Some veterans of the D-Day landings still have a difficult time describing what they saw, heard, or

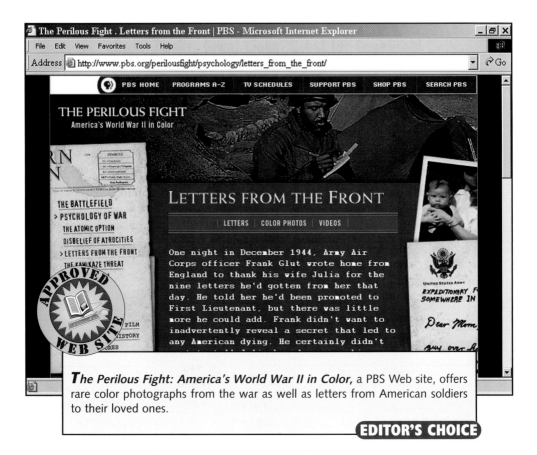

Address 🔗 http://www.pbs.org/perilousfight/psychology/letters_from_the_front/

THE PERILOUS FIGHT
America's World War II in Color

THE BATTLEFIELD
> PSYCHOLOGY OF WAR
THE ATOMIC OPTION
DISBELIEF OF ATROCITIES
> LETTERS FROM THE FRONT
THE KAMIKAZE THREAT

LETTERS FROM THE FRONT

| LETTERS | COLOR PHOTOS | VIDEOS |

One night in December 1944, Army Air Corps officer Frank Glut wrote home from England to thank his wife Julia for the nine letters he'd gotten from her that day. He told her he'd been promoted to First Lieutenant, but there was little more he could add. Frank didn't want to inadvertently reveal a secret that led to any American dying. He certainly didn't

The Perilous Fight: America's World War II in Color, a PBS Web site, offers rare color photographs from the war as well as letters from American soldiers to their loved ones.

EDITOR'S CHOICE

felt that momentous day. Others, like Commodore James Arnold of the U.S. Navy, have chosen to write about it. Arnold recalled his experience landing on the beaches of Normandy:

As the ramp lowered, I was shoved forward up to the knapsack in cold, oily water.

German 88s were pounding the beachhead. Two U.S. tanks were drawn up at the high-water line pumping them back into the Jerries [Germans]. I tried to run to get into the lee of these tanks. I realize now why the infantry likes to have tanks along in a skirmish. They offer a world of security to a man in open terrain who may have a terribly empty sensation in his guts. But my attempt to run was only momentary. Three feet of water is a real deterrent to rapid locomotion of the legs. As I stumbled into a runnel [channel], Kare picked me up. A little soldier following grabbed my other arm. Just for a moment he hung on. Then he dropped, blood spurting from a jagged hole torn by a sniper's bullet.[2]

Captain Joseph T. Dawson of the 16th Infantry Regiment also wrote about what it was like to land in France on that June morning in 1944:

The beach was a total chaos, with men's bodies everywhere, the wounded men crying, both in the water and on the shingle. We landed at high tide, when the water was right up to the shoreline, which was marked by a sharp-edged-crystal-like sand, like a small gravel, but very, very sharp. That was the only defilade [fortification] which was present . . . to give any protection from the fire above. That was where all the men who had landed earlier were present, except for a handful who had made their way forward, most of them being killed. The beach sounded like a beehive with the bullets flying around. You could hear them hit and you could hear them pass through the air.[3]

Escaping Death

In his memoirs, Joseph Steinbacher, a U.S. Army infantryman from Foley, Alabama, who served in the Pacific theater in New Guinea and the Philippines, recalls his first major combat experience. It was one

 *The view on D-Day: American soldiers descend the ramp of a Coast Guard landing vessel on June 6, 1944, and are met by heavy German machine-gun fire as they head to the beaches of Normandy.*

in which he narrowly escaped death in a foxhole. Foxholes were small holes dug in the ground to provide protection for soldiers from enemy fire.

The lieutenant stated that we would stay in these Japanese foxholes for the night. I didn't like the look of the whole setup, certainly not with those Japs up on top of Hill 255 waiting to pour fire down upon us sleeping in the cul-de-sac. I saluted the lieutenant and asked as politely as I could if it would be okay for several of us troopers to move up on the hillside. He replied that he didn't give a damn what I thought and where we dug in as long as we went up the hillside. . . .

Towards the morning as the sky was just beginning to get light, my eyes snapped open and I was instantly awake. Just then I heard a whistling sound, and a number of mortar shells, one after the other, came hurtling down into the cul-de-sac. We jumped up as soon as the explosions stopped, grabbed our equipment, and scrambled down the hill to see if we could help. Other soldiers . . . were just hauling out the last of the bodies. The lieutenant and sergeant were dead, along with three of the troopers, while another was badly wounded. I had been right about the spider holes; I didn't get much satisfaction from that fact.[4]

▶ Witnessing Death and Moving On

Later, Steinbacher ran into enemy fire along a road that had deep ditches on both sides and an open field beyond.

Most of us clambered down the right-hand ditch, then out of the other side to set up our perimeters in the open field and dig foxholes. Scattered mortar fire was falling . . . as we rushed to get a hole dug where we could at least have some protection. I looked over to where a friend, a red-headed private from the intelligence platoon was making dirt fly. Just as I glanced that way he received a direct hit from a mortar shell and was blown up right in front of my eyes.

 *After nearly two years of fighting in New Guinea and the Philippines, Sergeant Joseph Steinbacher of the 169th Infantry was told that he and his regiment would be part of a force to attack Japan, planned for November 1945. With the war's ending in September, the sergeant was spared that peril.*

When the soldier next to Steinbacher ran out of ammo, ammunition, for his M1, an automatic rifle, Steinbacher went to look for more.

After traveling a short distance I noticed a dead soldier sitting up against the back of the ditch. He had a well-filled ammo belt around his waist, and I immediately rushed over to pull off the belt. . . . I felt something slippery all over my hand, and paying no attention, finally was able to jerk the belt from behind the body. My hand was completely covered in the dead trooper's blood. I shuddered as I wiped my hand off as best I could on the soldier's uniform and hurried back to my place in the line.

The soldier grabbed a clip, shoving it into his M1. "Sorry about the blood," I said. [He replied] "No problem, makes the shells slip into the breach real easy."[5]

Joseph Steinbacher survived the war and was part of the American military force that occupied Japan after the war ended.

Horrible Images

The images of war's destruction were devastating to behold, no matter who was being killed. Robert Sherrod, a war correspondent in the Pacific, remembered the tenacity of one Japanese defender who met a terrible end:

A Marine jumped over the seawall and began throwing blocks of TNT into a coconut-log pillbox [place where weapons were stored]. Two more Marines scaled the seawall [with a flame-thrower]. As another charge of TNT boomed inside the pillbox, causing smoke and dust to billow out, a khaki-clad figure ran out from the side entrance. The flame thrower, waiting for him, caught him in its withering flame of intense fire. As soon as it touched him the Jap flared up like a piece of celluloid. He was dead instantly but the bullets in his cartridge belt exploded for a full sixty seconds after he had been charred almost to nothingness.[6]

THE HOME FRONT

No war is fought just on the battlefields, and World War II was no exception. The effort on the home front to support the troops abroad was crucial to their success. Many women stepped into jobs held by men before the war to keep the Allied war machine rolling.

Marie Brand Voltzke enlisted in the Navy WAVES—Women Accepted for Voluntary Emergency Service—to serve as a clerk in Washington, D.C. WAVES had to undergo a battery of tests and take an oath to protect the confidentiality of their assignments. They were told that they would be shot if they gave out any information on their work. Voltzke's first assignment was to add a group of numbers, but she had no idea what they were for. She described the job as "far from exciting," but things occurred that made her wonder what was *really* going on.

In the beginning there was only one other WAVE and our officer, Lt. Theriault. The section grew to an additional officer, more WAVEs, two sailors, and two civilian workers, a man and wife. The number on all shifts was the same, but the combinations varied. The work procedure was the same, but I assumed more difficult. Work that met a certain pattern went in one basket, otherwise into another basket.

In all my time in the service, Lt. Theriault was my favorite officer. On a midnight shift, I took work to him that did not follow the usual pattern. He became excited, and the commanding officer, who was off duty, was called in.

In a few days I was called to go to the Naval Department to receive a commendation. At that time I was a second class petty officer. My reward was that the time between second class and first class petty officer would be waived. However, I was required to take the regular first class exam. On February 19, 1944, I received a memo from Lt. (j.g.) Pond, an officer from

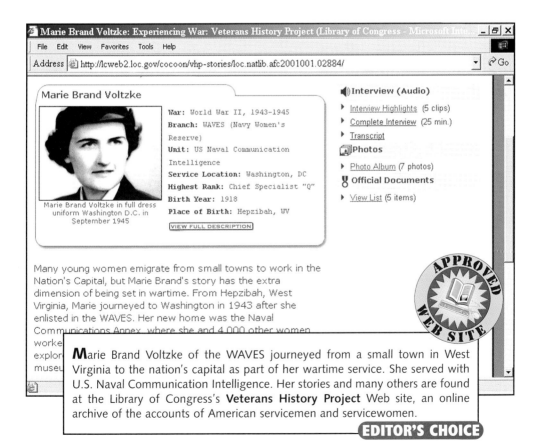

Marie Brand Voltzke: Experiencing War: Veterans History Project (Library of Congress - Microsoft Inte...

File Edit View Favorites Tools Help

Address http://lcweb2.loc.gov/cocoon/vhp-stories/loc.natlib.afc2001001.02884/

Marie Brand Voltzke

Marie Brand Voltzke in full dress uniform Washington D.C. in September 1945

War: World War II, 1943-1945
Branch: WAVES (Navy Women's Reserve)
Unit: US Naval Communication Intelligence
Service Location: Washington, DC
Highest Rank: Chief Specialist "Q"
Birth Year: 1918
Place of Birth: Hepzibah, WV

VIEW FULL DESCRIPTION

◀)) **Interview (Audio)**
▶ Interview Highlights (5 clips)
▶ Complete Interview (25 min.)
▶ Transcript
Photos
▶ Photo Album (7 photos)
Official Documents
▶ View List (5 items)

Many young women emigrate from small towns to work in the Nation's Capital, but Marie Brand's story has the extra dimension of being set in wartime. From Hepzibah, West Virginia, Marie journeyed to Washington in 1943 after she enlisted in the WAVES. Her new home was the Naval Communications Annex, where she and 4,000 other women worked...
explor...
museu...

APPROVED WEB SITE

Marie Brand Voltzke of the WAVES journeyed from a small town in West Virginia to the nation's capital as part of her wartime service. She served with U.S. Naval Communication Intelligence. Her stories and many others are found at the Library of Congress's **Veterans History Project** Web site, an online archive of the accounts of American servicemen and servicewomen.

EDITOR'S CHOICE

administration at the barracks, congratulating me on my promotion to Sp. Q. first class, stating I was first in the entire Annex. Our classification in the meantime had been changed to a new rating of Specialist Q. Consequently, I became the first Chief Sp. Q. on the station. My friends bought my chief's hat, emblem, and patches. All awaited to take my picture the next morning as I exited the barracks.

Arriving at work a few days later, both civilian workers were gone. We were never told the reason. I often wondered if they were spies.

To this day, I've never been enlightened as to what I accomplished or the results of our work in the Pacific Theater. I've never been notified of a reunion or if our work had been declassified.[1]

A Job to Be Proud Of

Cornelia Fort was a pilot with the WAFS, the Women's Auxiliary Ferrying Squadron. Her job was to transport airplanes for the Army. It was a job that she took great pride in, although she disagreed with the perception that most nonfliers had about the "glamour" of flying:

We get up in the cold dark in order to get to the airplanes by dawn. If the weather is good, we fly all day, usually without lunch. We wear heavy cumbersome flying suits and 30-pound parachutes. We are either cold or hot and you can't change clothes very well in the air. We get sunburns and windburns and if female your lipstick wears off and your hair gets straighter and straighter. You look forward all afternoon to the bath you will have and the steak. Well, we get the bath

but sometimes we are too tired to eat the steak and we fall wearily into bed.

Still, she took great satisfaction in her contribution to the war effort.

None of us can put into words why we fly. It is something different for each of us. I can't say exactly why I fly, but I 'know' why as I've never known anything in my life. . . .

For the first time we felt a part of something larger. I, for one, am profoundly grateful that my one talent, my only knowledge, flying, happens to be of

American women were pressed into service during World War II to build the nation's arsenal, from weapons to fighter planes. This poster of Rosie the Riveter, characterizing the powerful American woman working in wartime factories, is one of many from **Powers of Persuasion: Poster Art From World War II.**

EDITOR'S CHOICE

use to my country when it is needed. That's all the luck
I ever hope to have.[2]

On March 21, 1943, Cornelia Fort was killed in a
collision while transporting a plane. She was the
first female American military pilot to die in the line
of duty.

Women's contributions to the war effort extended beyond military duty. They took factory
jobs that before the war were held by men. They
helped build the planes, ships, and weapons needed
for the war. Women such as Rose Kaminski in
Milwaukee, Wisconsin, whose husband was serving
in the Navy, described her job in an ordnance, or
weapons, factory.

> We went into the factory and this gentleman came
> up and said, "Well, we're going to be hiring inspec-
> tors and we're also going to be needing several crane
> operators."
>
> My ears perked up right away because my step-
> father was a crane operator. I said to him, "Oh, I'd like
> to see what a crane looks like and what I'd have to do.
> I'd be really interested because my dad was a crane
> operator."
>
> So he took several of us and walked into the
> factory. And here was this great big ordnance plant
> with machines all lined up in rows. They were making
> great big howitzer barrels. Overhead were the cranes,
> and he showed us what we'd have to do. I thought,
> "Oh, is this what my father used to do?" I said, "I'd like
> to try and see if I can do it."
>
> He said, "Well you just have to learn how to work
> the crane, and all you'd have to do is pick up these

great big"—they're like grinders that would go in and thread the barrels of these big howitzers—"and you'd have to set them in, and then you'd just have to sit and wait until all of this goes through a procedure before you would take up and lift this part and move the gun barrel on a flatcar."

I thought, "Well, gee, that sounded pretty nice."[3]

▶ Prisoners of War in Their Own Country

Not all Americans were free to contribute to the war effort. Following the Japanese attack on Pearl Harbor, more than 120,000 Japanese Americans

A More Perfect Union: Japanese Americans & the U.S. Constitution chronicles the shameful treatment of Japanese Americans who were forced into internment camps during the war. The camp at Tule Lake, California, was the largest of the ten into which 120,000 people of Japanese heritage were forced after the United States declared war on Japan.

living on the West Coast were confined to internment camps, and most of them were American citizens or legal aliens. More than half of them were children. Perceived as a threat, in a climate of fear and racial prejudice, they were confined to these camps for up to four years, under armed guard and surrounded by barbed wire, through an executive order issued by President Franklin D. Roosevelt.

Nearly fifty years later, Congress passed the Civil Liberties Act of 1988, which acknowledged that the Japanese Americans had been interned unjustly, and reparations, or payments, of $20,000 were paid

Prints and Photographs Digital Item Display - fsa1992001581/PP - Microsoft Internet Explorer

File   Edit   View   Favorites   Tools   Help

Address   http://lcweb2.loc.gov/cgi-bin/query/i?pp/fsaall:@filreq((@field(NUMBER+@band(fsac+1a35337))+@field   Go

Women working for the Douglas Aircraft Company during the war install parts of the tail fuselage section of a B-17 bomber, nicknamed the Flying Fortress because it could withstand even the most vicious attacks. This image is from **Rosie Pictures: Select Images Relating to American Women Workers,** a Library of Congress site.

to each surviving person who had been held in the camps.

Mine Okubo, given the designation Citizen 13660, described the conditions of the camp where she and her daughter were held.

The loss of privacy was one of the great indignities suffered by evacuees.

My small daughter and I used to eat at a table where two little boys. . . ate with their mothers. They had become so uncontrollable that the mothers gave up, and let them eat as they pleased. . . .

We lined up for mail, for checks, for meals, for showers, for laundry tubs, for toilets, for clinic service, for movies. We lined up for everything.[4]

"Arsenal of Democracy"

Leaders gave speeches to keep up morale throughout the war. President Franklin D. Roosevelt was famous for his "fireside chats," speeches broadcast on radio. Even before the United States entered the war, Roosevelt began preparing Americans for America's eventual involvement:

The people of Europe who are defending themselves do not ask us to do their fighting. They ask us for the implements of war, the planes, the tanks, the guns, the freighters which will enable them to fight for their liberty and for our security. Emphatically we must get these weapons to them, get them to them in sufficient volume and quickly enough so that we and our children will be saved the agony and suffering of war which others have to endure. . . . We must be the great arsenal of democracy. . . . I call upon our people with absolute confidence that our common cause will greatly succeed.[5]

"Their Finest Hour"

The true master of morale was Prime Minister Winston Churchill of Great Britain. To rally his people after the fall of France, when England stood alone against Germany and Italy, Churchill stood before Parliament, Britain's governing body, and the British Empire and gave this stirring and defiant speech:

What General Weygand called the Battle of France is over. I expect that the Battle of Britain is about to begin. Upon this battle depends the survival of Christian civilization. . . . If we fail, then the whole world, including the United States, including all that we have known and cared for, will sink into the abyss of a new Dark Age made more sinister, and perhaps more protracted, by the lights of perverted science. Let us therefore brace ourselves to our duties and so bear ourselves that, if the British Empire and its Commonwealth last for a thousand years, men will still say, This was their finest hour.[6]

Chapter 7 ▶

LETTERS AND VOICES FROM THE OTHER SIDE

War is terrible no matter which side one fights for, and soldiers on opposing sides often have similar experiences. Harry Mielert, a German infantryman, wrote about what combat was like while he was serving in Russia.

> The Russians shot into [the town] with artillery, nearly all the houses were burning, in between large stores of munitions detonated and buildings and facilities were blown up by Pioneers. Everything roared, flamed, shook, cattle bellowed, soldiers searched through all the buildings, kegs of red wine were taken away on small panje wagons, here and there was drinking and singing, amid that again the explosions and the new fires roaring out. But the strangest thing is the colorful confusion. It is magnificent. All the barriers are broken. Anger roars through the all the cracks in the world.[1]

Werner Kortenhaus was in the 21st Panzer Division in France at the time of the D-Day landings in Normandy. Panzer divisions were made up of tanks with motorized infantry support. Kortenhaus

▲ *A German soldier carrying ammunition boxes in Belgium, December 1944. Nearly 20 million men served in the German armed forces during World War II.*

described the Allied invasion from a German soldier's point of view.

We made two attacks, one on the seventh of June and one on the ninth, and had a lot of losses— of our seventeen tanks, only one survived. The rest were destroyed. That had a big effect on us, and we sat around afterwards very crushed in spirits. It was now clear to us that we weren't going to do it, we weren't going to push the Allies back. The Allied attacks were too strong, particularly because of their air superiority.

I have one terrible memory. On 9 June we had attacked Escoville, an attack which only lasted a few minutes. There were infantry behind us, under covers, who were wounded and we began to reverse. The driver can only see in front of him and did not know they were there. We reversed over them, over our own infantry. Because they were wounded they couldn't move out of the way. One saw some terrible things.[2]

Kortenhaus also recalled lighter moments, such as one when a British tank crew surrendered.

Two English soldiers got out of the tank, they were wounded and gave themselves up. I imagine they had panicked because they had somehow lost their way and suddenly found themselves in the middle of so many tanks and then made a bad reaction. So of course we were interested to have a look inside an English tank, and inside I found a large thermos flask. My crew were very pleased because it was full of delicious hot coffee.

A few days later this thermos flask slipped out of my hands and broke—and I was really sworn at by the crew. The wireless operator always had to look after the provisions, and the thermos flask was a real prize. When I broke it I was much told off.[3]

▷ A German's Account of D-Day

Herbert Walther of the 12th SS Panzer Division was a tank commander whose unit tried to push back the Allied landing at Normandy. He wrote about being wounded and then captured by Allied forces:

My driver was burning. I had a bullet through the arm. I jumped on to a railway track and ran. They were firing down the embankment and I was hit in the leg. I made 100 meters, . . . it was as if I was hit in the back of the neck with a big hammer. A bullet had gone in beneath the ear and come out through the cheek.

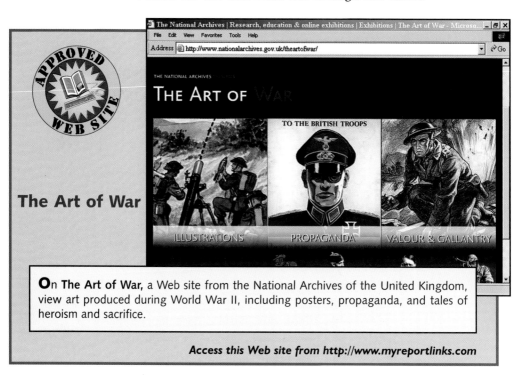

The Art of War

On **The Art of War,** a Web site from the National Archives of the United Kingdom, view art produced during World War II, including posters, propaganda, and tales of heroism and sacrifice.

Access this Web site from http://www.myreportlinks.com

I was choking on blood. There were two Americans looking down at me and two French soldiers who wanted to finish me off.[4]

Herbert Walther was not "finished off," however, and thirteen bullets were removed from his leg at the casualty station.

An Officer's Burden

Officers in all armies are responsible for the fate of their men. That responsibility often brings with it a heavy burden. Yanagida Eiichi was a thirty-three-year-old Japanese infantry lieutenant when he wrote this letter to his wife before he and his men shipped out from Japan. Seeing his men bid good-bye to wives and children made him realize how much he would worry about his own family.

Thank you for writing so often, and forgive me for not responding sooner. . . .

Yesterday, most of the work was completed. Today was visiting day, and confusion reigned. Some of the soldiers were holding babies in their arms. Others were leading small children by the hand as they headed out, perhaps for a brief excursion. Will my men be separated from their families for only a short time, or forever? When I see the innocent children, I get a lump in my throat. The knowledge that I am responsible for the fates of several dozen subordinates weighs heavily on my shoulders.

Is Kyoko feeling any better? I may be asking the impossible, but please do all you can to ensure that her illness is cured promptly, no matter how much it

Japanese soldiers taken prisoner of war in Guam bow their heads after hearing the news that Japan's leader, Emperor Hirohito, had unconditionally surrendered to the Allies on August 15, 1945.

costs. I worry about her all the time. Whatever the case, please take good care of her until I return. . . . [5]

Kyoko was Lieutenant Eiichi's daughter. Unfortunately, her father never returned—he was killed in action.

▶ Combat Humor

Soldiers on both sides tried to retain a sense of humor. The following are some instructions given to German soldiers going on leave so that they could once again fit into civilian life after the war. This advice is similar to the instructions given to American soldiers presented in Chapter Four.

> Curfew: If you forget your [house] key, try to open the door with the round-shaped object. Only in cases of extreme urgency use a grenade.
>
> Defense against Partisans: It is not necessary to ask civilians the password and open fire on receiving an unsatisfactory answer.
>
> Defense against Animals: Dogs with mines attached to them are a special feature of the Soviet Union. German dogs in the worst cases bite, but they do not explode. Shooting every dog you see, although recommended in the Soviet Union, might create a bad impression. . . .
>
> General: When on leave back in the Fatherland [Germany] take care not to talk about the paradise existence in the Soviet Union in case everybody wants to come here and spoil our idyllic comfort.[6]

▶ Lost Hope

There were times, of course, when desperation overcame humor. Bruno Kaliga, a German soldier fighting in Stalingrad, conveyed that hopelessness in a letter to his family as the German Army disintegrated around him:

 German troops await an attack in Russia, 1941.

My dear ones!

It is New Year's Eve, and when I think about home, my heart breaks. How miserable and hopeless everything is here. It's been four days since I had any bread. I am subsisting only on soup, for lunch. In the morning and in the evening, I have a swallow of coffee, and every two days I get about 100 grams of meat or some sardines in oil or a bit of cheese. . . . Day and night, we are attacked by planes, and the artillery fire never ends. If a miracle doesn't happen within the next few days, I will go down here. . . .

Sometimes I pray, and sometimes I curse my own fate. Everything is without purpose and without sense. . . . Will death come through a bomb or a grenade? Will it be sickness or chronic illness?

All of these questions overwhelm us to no end. And with it comes the constant longing to go home, and homesickness does indeed become a sickness. . . . I am without hope, and I ask you, don't cry too much when you receive the news that I am no more. Be good to each other, thank God for every day that's given to you, because at home, life is sweet.

With heartfelt love,

Yours,

Bruno[7]

It is unlikely that Bruno's family ever heard of his fate. Of the six hundred thousand German soldiers trapped in Stalingrad, five hundred thousand died, and of the one hundred thousand survivors that the Soviets captured, only about five thousand returned home after the war.[8]

A Survivor's Tale

Yamaoka Michiko was a fifteen-year-old schoolgirl in Hiroshima who was pressed into service during the war as a telephone operator. On August 6, 1945, as she was walking to work, she heard the buzzing of a bomber and looked up to see if she could spot it. When the blast occurred, sound ceased.

There was no sound. I felt something strong. It was terribly intense. I felt colors. It wasn't heat. You can't really say it was yellow, and it wasn't blue. At that moment I thought I would be the only one who would die. I said to myself, "Goodbye, Mom."

They say temperatures of seven thousand degrees centigrade hit me. You really can't say it washed over me. It's hard to describe. I simply fainted. I remember my body floating in the air. That was probably the blast, but I don't know how far I was blown. When I came to my senses, my surroundings were silent. There was no wind. I saw a slight thread-like light, so I felt I must be alive.

My clothes were burnt and so was my skin. I was in rags. I had braided my hair, but now it was like a lion's mane. There were people, barely breathing, trying to push their intestines back in. People with their legs wrenched off. Without heads. Or with faces burned and swollen out of shape. The scene I saw was a living hell.[9]

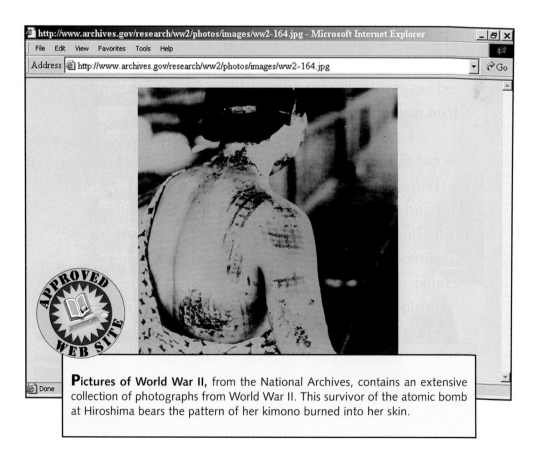

Pictures of World War II, from the National Archives, contains an extensive collection of photographs from World War II. This survivor of the atomic bomb at Hiroshima bears the pattern of her kimono burned into her skin.

▲ A cathedral is one of the few structures left standing in the devastated land-scape of Nagasaki after an atomic bomb was dropped on the Japanese city.

Yamaoka Michiko was less than a thousand yards from the place the atomic bomb hit when it was dropped on Hiroshima. Amazingly, she survived the blast and later traveled to the United States for plastic surgery to treat the horrible disfigurement she had suffered.

THE ROLE OF THE MEDIA

World War II saw the most extensive battlefield coverage by reporters of any war to its time. War correspondents had been around since the Crimean War in the 1840s, but the first United States war to be reported on was the Mexican-American War, from 1846 to 1848. Photography was in its infancy then, but by 1863, when the American Civil War erupted, the horrors of the battlefield were captured by the camera's lens. The Spanish-American War, in 1898, received even greater coverage, and during America's involvement in World War I, from 1917 through 1918, reporters spent time with American doughboys in the muddy, terrible trenches of Belgium and France.

▶ War Correspondents

In World War II, however, with the improved communications of radio, journalists could report more quickly on combat than ever before. Walter Cronkite, considered America's most trusted television anchor for nearly twenty years, first gained fame for his reporting from the battlefields of World

Correspondent Ernest Taylor Pyle, better known as Ernie, on board an aircraft carrier with American sailors in the Pacific. Pyle was a favorite of servicemen because he endured the same dangers they did.

War II as a correspondent for the wire service then known as United Press. Cronkite covered the Allied landings in North Africa and Sicily and the D-Day landings at Normandy. He also accompanied Allied bombers on missions over Germany.

Ernie Pyle, a reporter for the Scripps-Howard newspaper chain, became one of the most widely read correspondents because he captured the lives of average American soldiers through interviews. Those personal accounts helped readers feel that they knew what was really happening to their loved ones thousands of miles from home. Pyle, who ventured closer to the front for his stories than most reporters, made his subjects—the soldiers—feel as if he were one of them. Like too many of them, he was killed, shot by a sniper on the island of Ie Shima while covering the war in the Pacific.

One of the most famous war reporters of the Second World War was Edward R. Murrow, a CBS radio correspondent. He is remembered for his reports from London as German bombs flattened parts of the English capital all around him.

We are told today that the Germans believe Londoners, after a while, will rise up and demand a new government, one that will make peace with Germany. It's more probably that they'll rise up and murder a few German pilots who come down by parachute. The life of a parachutist would not be worth much in the East End of London tonight.

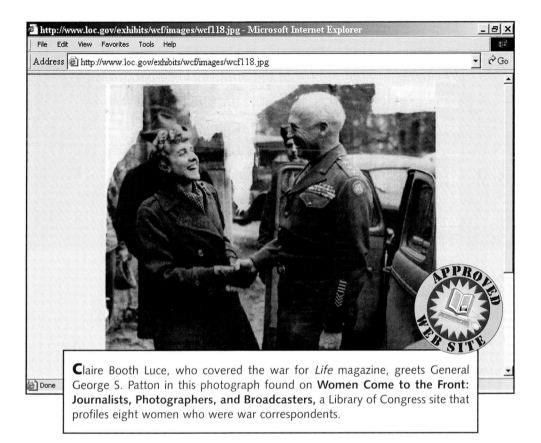

http://www.loc.gov/exhibits/wcf/images/wcf118.jpg - Microsoft Internet Explorer

File   Edit   View   Favorites   Tools   Help

Address   http://www.loc.gov/exhibits/wcf/images/wcf118.jpg   Go

Claire Booth Luce, who covered the war for *Life* magazine, greets General George S. Patton in this photograph found on **Women Come to the Front: Journalists, Photographers, and Broadcasters,** a Library of Congress site that profiles eight women who were war correspondents.

The politicians who called this a "people's war" were right, probably more right than they knew at the time. I've seen some horrible sights in this city during these days and nights, but not once have I heard man, woman, or child suggest that Britain throw in her hand.[1]

▶ Hollywood's Role

Hollywood movie studios joined in the war effort. Actors such as Clark Gable and Jimmy Stewart volunteered for military service. Many more did their part by supporting war-bond drives and rallies or giving free performances at military hospitals. Others toured with the United Service Organizations (USO), a nongovernmental group that provides support for troops at the front as well as their families back home. It was common to complain that the USO shows were held far enough behind the lines that the combat soldiers did not get to see them, but comedians Bob Hope and Jerry Colonna took their USO shows right up to the front lines. They earned the love, appreciation, and respect of the soldiers they entertained.[2]

Hollywood studios kept servicemen and civilians entertained with films that helped take their audiences' minds off the war for a while, but movies about the war were also popular, including *Thirty Seconds Over Tokyo,* starring Spencer Tracy, *Casablanca,* starring Humphrey Bogart, and *Mrs. Miniver,* starring Greer Garson. Wartime comedies such as *Buck Privates,* starring Bud Abbott and Lou Costello, *The Great Dictator,* starring Charlie Chaplin, and *Road to Morocco,* starring Bob Hope and Bing Crosby, kept audiences laughing and helped boost morale.[3]

▶ Decorated Ships and Planes

The Walt Disney Studios provided hours of animated short films and training films for the military. They also created emblems and mascots for many of the American submarines as a way of uniting the crews.[4]

Submarines were not the only war machines to be decorated with art. Early in the war, General

A People at War - Microsoft Internet Explorer

File   Edit   View   Favorites   Tools   Help

Address   http://www.archives.gov/exhibits/a_people_at_war/prelude_to_war/articles_prelude_to_war/flying_tigers.h ▼   Go

Done

A People at War, a National Archives site, presents archival images and documents of World War II. It includes this photograph of an American P-40 fighter plane, guarded by a Chinese soldier, bearing the distinctive shark's-teeth emblem of the Flying Tigers, a volunteer force led by American general Claire Chennault.

Claire Chennault's Flying Tigers, a volunteer air force serving in China, painted distinctive sharks' teeth on their fighter planes. Allied bombers began to be decorated with what was called nose art, which gave each plane an identity. Many carried paintings of pin-up girls, glamorous actresses of the day, next to the name of the plane.[5]

Cartoons

World War II inspired a number of popular cartoonists. Sergeant George Baker's *Sad Sack* appeared in

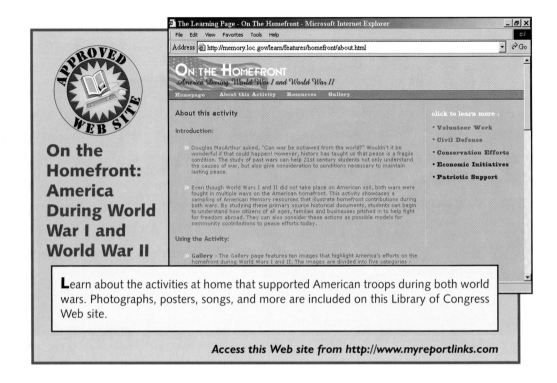

On the Homefront: America During World War I and World War II

The Learning Page - On The Homefront - Microsoft Internet Explorer

File   Edit   View   Favorites   Tools   Help

Address http://memory.loc.gov/learn/features/homefront/about.html   Go

ON THE HOMEFRONT
America During World War I and World War II

Homepage   About this Activity   Resources   Gallery

About this activity

Introduction:

click to learn more :

• Volunteer Work
• Civil Defense
• Conservation Efforts
• Economic Initiatives
• Patriotic Support

» Douglas MacArthur asked, "Can war be outlawed from the world?" Wouldn't it be wonderful if that could happen! However, history has taught us that peace is a fragile condition. The study of past wars can help 21st century students not only understand the causes of war, but also give consideration to conditions necessary to maintain lasting peace.

» Even though World Wars I and II did not take place on American soil, both wars were fought in multiple ways on the American homefront. This activity showcases a sampling of American Memory resources that illustrate homefront contributions during both wars. By studying these primary source historical documents, students can begin to understand how citizens of all ages, families and businesses pitched in to help fight for freedom abroad. They can also consider these actions as possible models for community contributions to peace efforts today.

Using the Activity:

» **Gallery** - The Gallery page features ten images that highlight America's efforts on the homefront during World Wars I and II. The images are divided into five categories -

Learn about the activities at home that supported American troops during both world wars. Photographs, posters, songs, and more are included on this Library of Congress Web site.

Access this Web site from http://www.myreportlinks.com

Yank Magazine and documented the frustrations and absurdities of the war as seen by an average soldier. More poignant and often with world-weary wit were Bill Mauldin's GIs (enlisted men) "Willie and Joe," who appeared in the U.S. Army newspaper *Stars and Stripes* and later in the book *Up Front*.[6]

Others were more critical of the war. An advertising artist, outraged at what was going on in Europe, published an editorial cartoon for New York's newspaper *PM*. What originally started as a one-time letter to the editor turned into a regular editorial cartooning job for the remainder of the war. The cartoonist, Theodor Seuss Geisel, became better known under the name Dr. Seuss.[7]

The Era's Music

Unlike the Civil War's "Battle Hymn of the Republic" or World War I's "Over There," World War II did not have a single song that represented the war to the American public. Music was, however, an important part of American life at the time. It was the era of Big Bands and swing music, performed by musicians such as Glenn Miller, Harry James, Count Basie, Tommy and Jimmy Dorsey, Benny Goodman, Duke Ellington, and others. The voices of Frank Sinatra, Bing Crosby, Ella Fitzgerald, and the Andrews Sisters, among many others, helped Americans forget about the hard times. Records were popular despite a government restriction on record production to save vital war materials such as wax and shellac.

Irving Berlin's "God Bless America" became almost a second national anthem, even though the song actually dated from World War I. Another Irving Berlin classic, "White Christmas," came to symbolize soldiers' desires to return to home, peace, and quiet. Originally written for the movie "Holiday Inn," Bing Crosby's recording sold over 20 million copies, and it remained the number-one selling song in the United States for decades.[8] "I'll Be Seeing You," also recorded by Bing Crosby, spoke of the longing for loved ones.

One of the era's most popular bandleaders became a casualty of the war. Glenn Miller joined the

▲ Bing Crosby entertains Allied troops in London, England, in August 1944. Crosby was one of the most popular singers of the era.

Army Specialists Corps and organized an orchestra to play for servicemen at home and abroad, giving up a lucrative career. Miller and his band were famous for such songs as "In the Mood," "When You Wish Upon a Star," "American Patrol," and "Moonlight Serenade." From England, where Miller and his band were playing for the soldiers stationed at military bases, he made arrangements to fly to Paris to set up a special radio broadcast for Christmas. He never made it—the single-engine plane he was on disappeared over the English Channel in December 1944.

"The Greatest Generation"

Books about the men and women who risked their lives in the Second World War remind us of their sacrifice.

In *The Greatest Generation,* which recounts the stories of American veterans of World War II, former news anchor Tom Brokaw summed up the extraordinary achievements of the "ordinary" American men and women who served their country and the world during the Second World War. They were part of what Brokaw calls "the greatest generation any society ever produced."

At a time in their lives when their days and nights should have been filled with innocent adventure, love, and the lessons of the workaday world, they were fighting in the most primitive conditions possible across the bloodied landscape of France, Belgium, Italy, Austria, and the coral islands of the Pacific. . . . They faced great odds and a late start, but they did not protest. They succeeded on every front. They won the war; they saved the world. They came home to joyous and short-lived celebrations and immediately began the task of rebuilding their lives.[9]

COMING HOME

When the war ended, American soldiers were excited to return to their civilian lives, although the reactions to the end of war differed greatly, and some were not even sure that the war was actually over.

Denton Crocker, a biologist from Massachusetts, was part of an Army unit made up of scientists and science students known as "bug chasers." His unit and others like it were formed to identify disease-carrying mosquitoes in the South Pacific, where malaria was considered as deadly to American troops as the enemy. Crocker, who spent the war in the jungles of New Guinea, the Dutch East Indies, and the Philippines, described his voyage home from Japan.

I remember the hold crammed with tiers of bunks, and water of condensation from the human cargo of many "sardines" streaming down the inside of the cold hull. I can also recall standing watch outside in the bow in a dense, cold mist, having been instructed to keep an eye out for mines, which were reported to have come loose from their moorings. We arrived in the U.S. at San Pedro, CA. From there I was carried by troop train to Ft. Devens, MA. That trip too is largely blank, but I do remember annoyance at not knowing

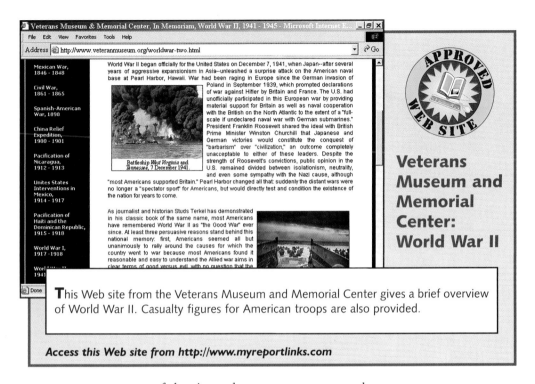

Veterans Museum & Memorial Center, In Memoriam, World War II, 1941 - 1945 - Microsoft Internet E...

File   Edit   View   Favorites   Tools   Help

Address http://www.veteranmuseum.org/worldwar-two.html   ▼ Go

Mexican War,
1846 - 1848

Civil War,
1861 - 1865

Spanish-American
War, 1898

China Relief
Expedition,
1900 - 1901

Pacification of
Nicaragua,
1912 - 1913

Unites States
Interventions in
Mexico,
1914 - 1917

Pacification of
Haiti and the
Dominican Republic,
1915 - 1918

World War I,
1917 - 1918

World War II,
1941

World War II began officially for the United States on December 7, 1941, when Japan--after several years of aggressive expansionism in Asia--unleashed a surprise attack on the American naval base at Pearl Harbor, Hawaii. War had been raging in Europe since the German invasion of Poland in September 1939, which prompted declarations of war against Hitler by Britain and France. The U.S. had unofficially participated in this European war by providing material support for Britain as well as naval cooperation with the British on the North Atlantic to the extent of a "full-scale if undeclared naval war with German submarines." President Franklin Roosevelt shared the ideal with British Prime Minister Winston Churchill that Japanese and German victories would constitute the conquest of "barbarism" over "civilization," an outcome completely unacceptable to either of these leaders. Despite the strength of Roosevelt's convictions, public opinion in the U.S. remained divided between isolationism, neutrality, and even some sympathy with the Nazi cause, although "most Americans supported Britain." Pearl Harbor changed all that: suddenly the distant wars were no longer a "spectator sport" for Americans, but would directly test and condition the existence of the nation for years to come.

Battleship West Virginia and Tennessee, 7 December 1941.

As journalist and historian Studs Terkel has demonstrated in his classic book of the same name, most Americans have remembered World War II as "the Good War" ever since. At least three persuasive reasons stand behind this national memory: first, Americans seemed all but unanimously to rally around the causes for which the country went to war because most Americans found it reasonable and easy to understand the Allied war aims in clear terms of good versus evil, with no question that the

APPROVED
WEB SITE

Veterans Museum and Memorial Center: World War II

Done

This Web site from the Veterans Museum and Memorial Center gives a brief overview of World War II. Casualty figures for American troops are also provided.

Access this Web site from http://www.myreportlinks.com

most of the time where we were, even what state we were in. Somewhere in the plains a wheel of one of the train cars jumped off the track and it was some hours before we could continue. During the delay, I walked a mile or two away from the train along a dirt road, trying to get a feel for the place, but if I knew then where it was, I now have forgotten. It was my great good fortune to arrive home on December 23 and so to be able to celebrate Christmas with my family and my wife-to-be. JM [Jean-Marie] and I were married on February 23.[1]

Donald Spencer of the Army Air Corps was a gunner on a bomber that flew missions over Germany. One of his sisters turned his letters into a memoir, which she narrated. She describes her brother's return to the United States.

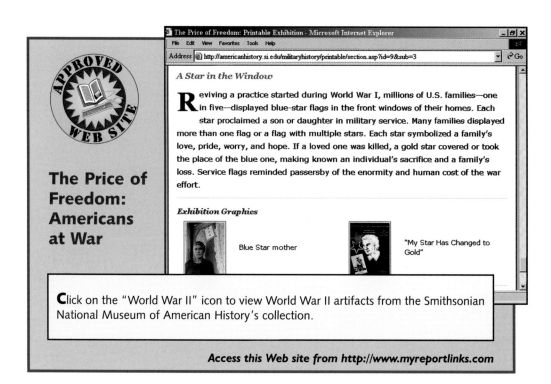

The Price of Freedom: Americans at War

The Price of Freedom: Printable Exhibition - Microsoft Internet Explorer

File   Edit   View   Favorites   Tools   Help

Address http://americanhistory.si.edu/militaryhistory/printable/section.asp?id=9&sub=3

A Star in the Window

Reviving a practice started during World War I, millions of U.S. families—one in five—displayed blue-star flags in the front windows of their homes. Each star proclaimed a son or daughter in military service. Many families displayed more than one flag or a flag with multiple stars. Each star symbolized a family's love, pride, worry, and hope. If a loved one was killed, a gold star covered or took the place of the blue one, making known an individual's sacrifice and a family's loss. Service flags reminded passersby of the enormity and human cost of the war effort.

Exhibition Graphics

Blue Star mother

"My Star Has Changed to Gold"

Click on the "World War II" icon to view World War II artifacts from the Smithsonian National Museum of American History's collection.

Access this Web site from http://www.myreportlinks.com

The ship sailed from Le Havre on November 4, 1945. The second day out, they ran into a very bad North Atlantic storm. Waves of fifty and sixty feet pounded them for three days and two nights. Ninety percent of the troops and crew aboard were seasick. Don and a new friend did not get sick, despite the odors in their compartment.

They sailed into New York harbor on the morning of November 11, Armistice Day, 1945. They sailed by the Statue of Liberty with the decks jammed shoulder to shoulder, and all aboard cheering. Farther up the harbor with the skyscrapers of New York City in the background they were met by fireboats that were spouting water into the air.

Several motorized barges pulled up alongside the ship with bands aboard them playing, and on one of the barges the Rockette dancers were doing

their famous dance kicks. It was quite an unexpected welcome. New York City was celebrating Armistice Day and the arrival of troop ships from Europe, and just by chance they became part of it.[2]

Joseph Steinbacher of the U.S. Army was not sent home immediately. He was stationed with the forces occupying Japan, where he was surprised to find that the Japanese civilians did not hate him as a

▲ *This photograph of a sailor in New York City, sweeping a nurse into his arms to celebrate the war's end with a kiss, is one of the most famous images of its time. Those Americans lucky enough to return home after World War II raised families, found or returned to jobs, and tried to rebuild their lives.*

member of a conquering army. When he was finally able to leave for home, he became ill.

I was set for a nice, quiet trip home but no luck. We no sooner sailed then I came down with a terrible case of malaria. They had only something called bismuth pills and absolutely nothing to help me, so I suffered the daily bout with the malaria all the way across the Pacific to Seattle. I checked into a hospital at Fort Lawton in Seattle, got dosed up well with quinine, and was okay in a few days.

When Steinbacher recovered, he was given the chance to reenlist, but it was an opportunity he refused.

One day, I was called in to a little office where a corporal sat behind a desk. He shoved a couple of documents in front of me and told me to sign one of them. I asked what the documents were and he said one set were reenlistment papers and the other discharge papers. If I would reenlist, they would increase my rank to staff sergeant. The Army was still trying, but I wasn't buying. I didn't have any more lives to give my country. I signed the discharge papers and was no longer a member of the armed forces. It was the month of January in this year of our Lord, 1946.[3]

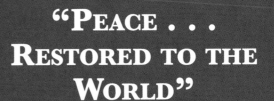

Chapter 10

"PEACE . . . RESTORED TO THE WORLD"

World War II was the largest and deadliest conflict the world has ever seen. Although it is impossible to know exactly how many lives were lost during the Second World War, it is estimated that fifty-five million people were killed, and millions more were displaced. One thing is certain: The world was changed drastically.[1]

As Allied forces pushed into the German heartland, they discovered the full measure of the Nazis' crimes. Six million Jews and more than 20 million Slavs, gypsies, homosexuals, and other people that the Germans considered "undesirable" were herded into factories of death and systematically executed.[2] Auschwitz, Dachau, Buchenwald, Bergen-Belsen, and Treblinka were some of the concentration camps in which the Nazis staged the genocide known as the Holocaust.

▷ Judgment at Nuremberg

Immediately following the war, the Allies set up a war crimes tribunal in Nuremberg (in German, Nürnberg), Germany. There, German officials

The U.S. Ninth Army liberated the German concentration camp at Wobbelin in May 1945, finding many of its former prisoners in desperate condition.

accused of taking part in the slaughter of the Holocaust were tried. German military figures responsible for the atrocities committed on the eastern front were tried as well. After a year of trials, the tribunal at Nuremberg sentenced twelve defendants to death and three to life terms in prison. The highest-ranking surviving Nazi, Hermann Göring, cheated the hangman's noose by committing suicide just before he was to be executed.[3]

▶ A Divided Germany

The Nuremburg trials represented the last real cooperation between all the Allies. The United States, Britain, and France began to find themselves increasingly distrustful and at odds with the Communist government of the Soviet Union. Germany was divided into four sectors, one for each of the "Big Four." The British, French, and American sectors were combined into the Federal Republic of Germany, or West Germany, a democracy, while the Soviet sector became the German Democratic Republic, a Communist state.[4] Berlin was also divided into free West Berlin and Communist East Berlin. This division served as the focal point for several crises during the Cold War, the period of tension and mistrust between the United States and the Soviet Union that began after World War II and continued until 1991. A Soviet blockade of Berlin, from June 24, 1948, to May 11, 1949, was only relieved by an airlift operation mounted by the

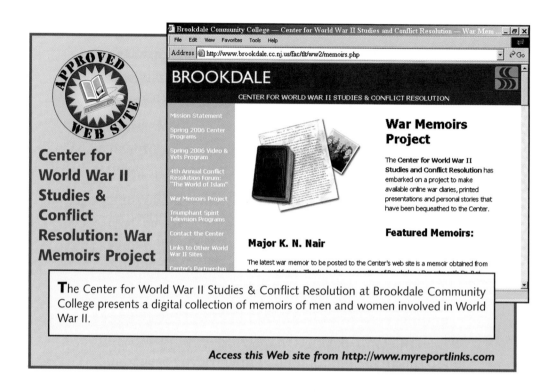

Brookdale Community College — Center for World War II Studies and Conflict Resolution — War Mem ...

File   Edit   View   Favorites   Tools   Help

Address http://www.brookdale.cc.nj.us/fac/tlt/ww2/memoirs.php

BROOKDALE

CENTER FOR WORLD WAR II STUDIES & CONFLICT RESOLUTION

Mission Statement

Spring 2006 Center Programs

Spring 2006 Video & Vets Program

4th Annual Conflict Resolution Forum: "The World of Islam"

War Memoirs Project

Triumphant Spirit Television Programs

Contact the Center

Links to Other World War II Sites

Center's Partnership

War Memoirs Project

The **Center for World War II Studies and Conflict Resolution** has embarked on a project to make available online war diaries, printed presentations and personal stories that have been bequeathed to the Center.

Featured Memoirs:

Major K. N. Nair

The latest war memoir to be posted to the Center's web site is a memoir obtained from

Center for World War II Studies & Conflict Resolution: War Memoirs Project

The Center for World War II Studies & Conflict Resolution at Brookdale Community College presents a digital collection of memoirs of men and women involved in World War II.

Access this Web site from http://www.myreportlinks.com

United States and other Allies that brought supplies to a starving people. The building of the Berlin Wall in 1961 became a tangible symbol of the conflict and division of Germany. Germany remained divided until the German Democratic Republic collapsed in 1989, and East Germany and West Germany were reunified.

▶ A World Divided

Germany was not the only place divided following the war. The political maneuvering of the Cold War between the Soviets and the western powers involved no shooting, but the entire world became caught up in it, aligning with one side or the other over the next forty years.[5] Europe was divided between democratic and Communist states. Countries occupied by the Soviets were transformed into Communist states like the Soviet Union. Poland, Czechoslovakia, Hungary, Yugoslavia, Bulgaria, Albania, and Romania only became democracies after the collapse of the Soviet Union.

Plans for Peace

It took years for most of Europe to recover from the destruction caused by the war. In 1947, the United States set up a plan to rebuild Europe. It became known as the Marshall Plan because General George C. Marshall, then secretary of state, oversaw it. The Marshall Plan provided money to rebuild European industry and to get the Europeans on their feet again.

To prevent the outbreak of another world war, in 1945 the international community created the United Nations as an organization to mediate problems between nations and maintain peace. The United Nations was also intended to help dismantle the existing empires of Britain, France, and Italy, and to assist new nations.

Postwar Japan and China

Like Germany, Japan was also occupied by the Allies after the war, but unlike Germany, Japan was occupied by American forces and kept intact. The American occupation of Japan was far less harsh

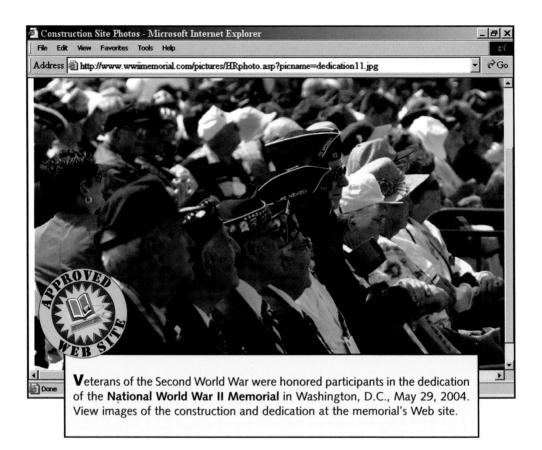

Veterans of the Second World War were honored participants in the dedication of the **National World War II Memorial** in Washington, D.C., May 29, 2004. View images of the construction and dedication at the memorial's Web site.

than the occupation of Germany, and the Japanese economy recovered. The Japanese military was limited so that it would not become a power once again. Without the burden of spending a great deal of money on its military, Japan reemerged as an industrial power and the leader for the economic development of the rest of East Asia.[6]

Final Words

On September 2, 1945, at the signing ceremony on the battleship USS *Missouri* that marked the formal end of World War II, General Douglas MacArthur gave this short speech:

> We are gathered here, representatives of the major warring powers, to conclude a solemn agreement whereby peace may be restored. The issues, involving divergent ideals and ideologies, have been determined on the battlefields of the world and hence are not for our discussion or debate. Nor is it for us here to meet, representing as we do a majority of the people of the earth, in a spirit of distrust, malice or hatred. But rather it is for us, both victors and vanquished to rise to that higher dignity which alone befits the sacred purposes we are about to serve, committing all our peoples unreservedly to faithful compliance with the understandings they are here formally to assume.
>
> It is my earnest hope that from this solemn occasion a better world shall emerge. A world dedicated to the dignity of man. The terms and conditions upon which surrender of the Japanese Imperial forces is here to be given and accepted are contained in the instrument of surrender before you.
>
> Let us pray that peace be now restored to the world, and that God preserve it always.
>
> These proceedings are closed.[7]

They closed only after more than 405,000 Americans had given their lives and nearly 700,000 had been wounded. The words of those who chose to tell or write about their experiences during World War II, however, will live forever.

Report Links

The Internet sites described below can be accessed at http://www.myreportlinks.com

▶**The Perilous Fight: America's World War II in Color**
Editor's Choice This Web site provides a rare collection of color photos from World War II.

▶**Voices of World War II: Experiences From the Front and at Home**
Editor's Choice This Web site provides an extensive World War II-era audio collection.

▶**Battle Lines: Letters From America's Wars**
Editor's Choice This Web site contains a sampling of letters written by American soldiers.

▶**Powers of Persuasion: Poster Art From World War II**
Editor's Choice View a World War II poster collection on this site.

▶*American Experience: D-Day*
Editor's Choice Read about the Allied invasion at Normandy on June 6, 1944.

▶**Veterans History Project**
Editor's Choice This Library of Congress site presents first-person accounts of American veterans of war.

▶*American Experience: Battle of the Bulge*
Learn about the biggest and bloodiest single battle that American soldiers ever fought.

▶**The Art of War**
View images of the war produced by British artists in this collection from the United Kingdom.

▶**The Avalon Project at Yale Law School: World War II Documents**
On this site, read the text of official documents produced during World War II.

▶**Center for World War II Studies & Conflict Resolution: War Memoirs Project**
Read this collection of personal memoirs from participants of World War II.

▶**Churchill and the Great Republic**
Learn about Winston Churchill and World War II on this site.

▶**Digitized Primary American History Sources**
View a collection of primary sources of American history.

▶**Dwight D. Eisenhower Presidential Library: D-Day**
The Eisenhower presidential archive presents primary source materials about D-Day.

▶**Franklin D. Roosevelt Presidential Library and Museum: The "Special Relationship"**
Learn about the relationship between Franklin D. Roosevelt and Winston Churchill during World War II.

▶**Gerald W. Thomas in World War II: An Exhibition**
Read the letters of a Navy pilot during the war.

Report Links

The Internet sites described below can be accessed at
http://www.myreportlinks.com

▶**German Propaganda Archive: Nazi Propaganda: 1933–1945**
Browse this collection of Nazi propaganda from World War II.

▶**A More Perfect Union: Japanese Americans & the U.S. Constitution**
Learn about the internment of Japanese Americans during World War II.

▶**National World War II Memorial**
Learn about the World War II Memorial in Washington, D.C.

▶**Northwestern University Library: World War II Poster Collection**
View Northwestern University's collection of World War II posters on this site.

▶**On the Homefront: America During World War I and World War II**
This Web site provides resources on the war effort at home during both world wars.

▶**Our Documents: Surrender of Japan (1945)**
Read the text of Japan's surrender, which ended the war.

▶**A People at War**
Learn about the soldiers and civilians who served the United States during World War II.

▶**Perry-Castañeda Library Map Collection: World War II Maps**
View maps from World War II on this site.

▶**Pictures of World War II**
Browse through World War II photos on this Web site.

▶**The Price of Freedom: Americans at War**
View World War II artifacts from the National Museum of American History.

▶**Rosie Pictures: Select Images Relating to American Women Workers**
View images of America's women who contributed to the war effort.

▶**Today in History: December 7**
Learn more about the Japanese attack that brought America into World War II.

▶**Veterans Museum and Memorial Center: World War II**
Read a brief overview of the war on this Web site dedicated to veterans.

▶**Wars and Conflict: World War Two**
Learn about World War II on this BBC Web site.

▶**Women Come to the Front: Journalists, Photographers, and Broadcasters**
Read about eight courageous women who were at the front in World War II.

Aryan—In the Nazi belief system, a Caucasian considered ethnically superior to other races.

Atlantic Wall—The German defenses protecting the western coast of France and Belgium from potential Allied invasion. The defenses were successfully breached by the D-Day landings of June 6, 1944.

blitzkrieg—"Lightning war" in German. It was warfare based on the speed of air superiority, surprise, highly mobile tanks, and motorized infantry to cut off an opposing army's communications and supply to create confusion.

chancellor—The head of government in some parliamentary democracies.

commandos—Formed by the British and named after South African soldiers of the Boer War, commandos were the first Special Forces unit and the forerunners of the U.S. Army Rangers. Commandos were trained for amphibious assaults and raids.

coxswain—The person in charge of a ship's boat and crew and usually the person who steers.

D-Day—The assault on northwest Europe by British, Canadian, and American soldiers on June 6, 1944, with troops landing on the beaches of Normandy in northwestern France.

European theater—The part of World War II fought in Europe.

Fascist—A member or supporter of the Fascist party in Italy led by the dictator Benito Mussolini from 1922 to 1943.

Greater East Asia Co-prosperity Sphere—Initially designed to be a defensive perimeter, the Greater East Asia Co-prosperity Sphere was essentially the Japanese Empire with a name that was intended to sound appealing to native Asian peoples living in European-controlled colonies. Its intent was to undermine the British, French, Dutch, and American forces in those colonies.

kamikaze—Japanese suicide pilots who tried to fly their planes into enemy ships. They inflicted serious damage on the United States fleet at the battles of Leyte Gulf, Iwo Jima, and Okinawa.

Luftwaffe—The German Air Force.

Nazi—A member of Germany's National Socialist Workers' party, which came into power in 1933 under Adolf Hitler.

Operation Market Garden—The Allied code name for a ground and air plan to seize bridges over the Rhine River.

Operation Overlord—The Allied code name for the D-Day invasion of Western Europe.

Operation Torch—The Allied code name for the campaign in North Africa, led by General Dwight Eisenhower.

Pacific theater—The campaigns of World War II fought in Asia and islands in the Pacific.

panzer—German for "armored," panzers were German tanks and also the name of tank divisions. The term is short for "Panzer Kampf Wagon."

reparations—Payments made by a defeated country in a war as compensation demanded by the victors in that war.

Rhineland—A region in western Germany bordering the Rhine River that was demilitarized by the Treaty of Versailles and then occupied by the Nazis in 1936.

samurai—A Japanese warrior of the aristocracy.

Siegfried Line—A line of German fortifications built by Hitler that extended for nearly four hundred miles along Germany's western border.

strafer—A machine-gun or cannon attack from a low-flying aircraft.

U-boat—Slang for a German submarine, from the German *Unterseeboot,* literally, "undersea boat."

What Are Primary Sources?

1. The Library of Congress, *Experiencing War: Stories From the Veterans History Project,* "D-Day Beyond the Beach: Tracy Sugarman," n.d., <http://memory.loc.gov/cocoon/vhp-stories/loc.natlib.afc2001001 .05440/> (March 6, 2006).

Chapter 1. "This Is No Drill!"

1. Nigel Fountain, ed., *WWII: The People's Story* (Pleasantville, N.Y.: Reader's Digest/Michael O'Mara Books, 2003), p. 111.

2. Henry Berry, *This Is No Drill! Living Memories of the Attack on Pearl Harbor* (New York: The Berkley Publishing Group, 2001), p. 163. "THIS IS NO DRILL!" LIVING MEMORIES OF THE ATTACK ON PEARL HARBOR by Henry Berry, copyright © 1992 by Henry Berry. Used by permission of Berkley Publishing Group, a division of Penguin Group (USA) Inc.

3. Ibid., p. 191.

4. Ibid., p. 166.

5. Franklin D. Roosevelt, *President Franklin D. Roosevelt's Address to a Joint Session of Congress Asking for a Declaration of War Against Japan,* National Archives and Records Administration, December 8, 1941, <http://www.archives.gov/legislative/features/day-of-infamy /index.html> (April 17, 2006).

Chapter 2. A Brief History of the War in Europe

1. Stefan Lorant, *Sieg Heil! (Hail to Victory): An Illustrated History of Germany from Bismarck to Hitler* (New York: W. W. Norton & Company, Inc., 1974), p. 106.

2. Ibid., p. 130.

3. Ibid., p. 125.

4. Ibid., p. 58.

5. Adolf Hitler, *Mein Kampf* (New York: Houghton Mifflin, 1999), p. 373.

6. Sir Max Hastings, *The Second World War: A World in Flames* (Oxford, U.K.: Osprey Publishing Ltd., 2004), p. 33.

7. Ibid.

8. Lorant, pp. 104–105.

9. Hastings, pp. 35–36.

10. Lorant, pp. 264–266.

11. C.L. Sulzberger, *The American Heritage Picture History of World War II* (Washington, D.C.: American Heritage Publishing: 1966), pp. 50–51.

12. Lorant, p. 123.

13. Hastings, p. 165.

14. Sulzberger, p. 58.

15. Hastings, pp. 60–61.

16. Sir John Keegan, *The Second World War*: A World in Flames (New York: Penguin Books, 1989), pp. 47–49.

17. Ibid., p. 49.

18. Ibid., pp. 50–51.

19. Hastings, p. 67.

20. Ibid., p. 75.

21. Keegan, p. 87.

22. Hastings, p. 78.

23. Ibid., p. 81.

24. Ibid.

25. Hastings, p. 83.

26. Keegan, pp. 170–171.

27. Ibid., p. 235.

28. Hastings, pp. 326–328.

29. Sir John Keegan, *The Rand McNally Encyclopedia of World War II* (New York: Rand McNally & Company, 1981), p. 73.

30. Keegan, *The Second World War,* pp. 336–337.

31. Ibid., p. 340.

32. Ibid., p. 343.

33. Sulzberger, p. 301.

34. Keegan, *The Second World War,* pp. 349–350.

35. Hastings, p. 385.

36. Ibid., pp. 396–397.

37. Ibid., p. 407.

38. Sulzberger, p. 573.

39. Ibid., p. 557.

Chapter 3. A Brief History of the War in the Pacific

1. John Costello, *The Pacific War, 1941–1945* (New York: Quill, 1981), pp. 14–15.

2. Sir Max Hastings, *The Second World War: A World in Flames* (Oxford, U.K.: Osprey Publishing Ltd., 2004), p. 229.

3. Costello, p. 52.

4. C.L. Sulzberger, *The American Heritage Picture History of World War II* (Washington, D.C.: American Heritage Publishing, 1966), p. 145.

5. Hastings, p. 241.

6. Ibid., pp. 248–249.

7. Costello, pp. 235–237.

8. Ibid., p. 263.

9. Ibid., pp. 307–309.

10. Hastings, p. 271.

11. Sulzberger, pp. 329–330.

12. Hastings, p. 264.

13. Costello, pp. 469–470.

14. Hastings, p. 273.

15. Ibid., pp. 276–277.

16. Ibid., p. 280.

17. Costello, pp. 587–588.

18. Ibid., pp. 589–593.

Chapter 4. A Soldier's Life

1. Tom Wiener, ed., *Voices of War: Stories of Service From the Home Front and the Front Lines* (Washington, D.C.: The National Geographic Society, 2004), p. 64.

2. Ibid., p. 67.

3. Ibid., p. 71.

4. Andrew Carroll, *Behind the Lines: Powerful and Revealing American and Foreign War Letters—And One Man's Search to Find Them* (New York: Scribner, 2005), pp. 277–278.

5. Ibid., p. 250.

6. Wiener, p. 94.

Chapter 5. Under Fire

1. C.L. Sulzberger, *The American Heritage Picture History of World War II* (Washington, D.C.: American Heritage Publishing, 1966), p. 540.

2. Jon E. Lewis, ed., *D-Day As They Saw It* (New York: Carroll & Graf Publishers, 2004), p. 100. Used with permission.

3. Ibid., p. 104.

4. Tom Wiener, ed., *Voices of War: Stories of Service From the Home Front and the Front Lines* (Washington, D.C.: The National Geographic Society, 2004), pp. 128–129.

5. Ibid., pp. 129–130.

6. Sir John Keegan, *The Second World War* (New York, Penguin Books, 1989), p. 303.

Chapter 6. The Home Front

1. Jon E. Lewis, ed., *D-Day As They Saw It* (New York: Carroll & Graf Publishers, 2004), pp. 224–225. Used with permission.

2. Emily Yellin, *Our Mothers' War: American Women at Home and at the Front During World War II* (New York: The Free Press, 2004), p. 157. Reprinted with the permission of The Free Press, a Division of Simon & Schuster Adult Publishing Group. Copyright © 2004 by Emily Yellin. All rights reserved.

3. Nigel Fountain, ed., *WWII: The People's Story* (Pleasantville, N.Y.: Reader's Digest/Michael O'Mara Books, 2003), pp. 216–217.

4. The Smithsonian Institution, National Museum of American History, *A More Perfect Union—Japanese Americans and the U.S. Constitution;* "Section IV, Life Behind Barbed Wire: The Internment Experience," n.d., <http://americanhistory.si.edu/perfectunion/resources/touring.html#SECTION4> (March 5, 2006).

5. Thomas R. Flagel, *The History Buff's Guide to World War II* (Nashville: Cumberland House Publishing, Inc., 2005), p. 65.

6. Ibid., p. 63.

Chapter 7. Letters and Voices From the Other Side

1. Stephen G. Fritz, *Frontsoldaten*: *The German Soldier in World War II* (Lexington: The University Press of Kentucky, 1995), p. 151.

2. Jon E. Lewis, ed., *D-Day As They Saw It* (New York: Carroll & Graf Publishers, 2004), pp. 195–196. Used with permission.

3. Ibid., pp. 215 216.

4. Ibid., p. 271.

5. Andrew Carroll, *Behind the Lines: Powerful and Revealing American and Foreign War Letters—And One Man's Search to Find Them* (New York: Scribner, 2005), pp. 87–88.

6. Ibid., p. 278.

7. Ibid., pp. 161–162.

8. Ibid., p. 162.

9. Haruko Tayo Cook and Theodore F. Cook, *Japan at War: An Oral History* (New York: The New Press, 1992), pp. 384–385.

Chapter 8. The Role of the Media

1. C.L. Sulzberger, *The American Heritage Picture History of World War II* (Washington, D.C.: American Heritage Publishing, 1966), p. 114.

2. Gerald F. Linderman, *The World Within War: America's Combat Experience in World War II* (Cambridge, Mass.: Harvard University Press, 1999), p. 315.

3. Sulzberger, p. 476.

4. Keith Wheeler, *War Under the Pacific* (Alexandria, Va.: Time-Life Books, 1980), p. 45.

5. Keith Wheeler, *Bombers Over Japan* (Alexandria, Va.: Time-Life Books, 1982), pp. 172–173.

6. Sulzberger, p. 400.

7. Richard H. Minear, *Dr. Seuss Goes to War: The World War II Editorial Cartoons of Theodor Seuss Geisel* (New York: The New York Press, 1999), pp. 10–16.

8. Thomas R. Flagel, *The History Buff's Guide to World War II* (Nashville: Cumberland House Publishing, Inc., 2005), pp. 181–185.

9. Tom Brokaw, *The Greatest Generation* (New York: Random House, 1998), xxvii.

Chapter 9. Coming Home

1. Tom Wiener, ed., *Voices of War: Stories of Service From the Home Front and the Front Lines* (Washington, D.C.: The National Geographic Society, 2004), p. 253.

2. Ibid., p. 261.

3. Ibid., pp. 260–261.

Chapter 10. "Peace . . . Restored to the World"

1. Sir Max Hastings, *The Second World War: A World in Flames* (Oxford, U.K.: Osprey Publishing Ltd., 2004), p. 463.

2. Ibid., p. 433.

3. C.L. Sulzberger, *The American Heritage Picture History of World War II* (Washington, D.C.: American Heritage Publishing, 1966), p. 624.

4. Hastings, pp. 458–459.

5. Ibid., 453–458.

6. Ibid., pp. 451–452.

7. Desmond Flower and James Reeves, *The War 1939–1945: A Documentary History* (Cambridge, Mass.: Da Capo Press, 1997), p. 1039.

Further Reading

Barr, Gary E. *World War II Home Front.* Chicago: Heinemann Library, 2004.

Bradley, James, with Ron Powers. *Flags of Our Fathers: Heroes of Iwo Jima.* New York: Delacorte Press, 2001.

Colman, Penny. *Where the Action Was: Women War Correspondents in World War II.* New York: Crown Publishers, 2002.

Giblin, James Cross. *The Life and Death of Adolf Hitler.* New York: Clarion Books, 2002.

Isserman, Maurice. *World War II.* New York: Facts On File, 2003.

Kuhn, Betsy. *Angel of Mercy: The Army Nurses of World War II.* New York: Atheneum Books for Young Readers, 1999.

Nardo, Don. *Pearl Harbor.* San Diego: Greenhaven Press, 2005.

———. *World War II.* San Diego: Greenhaven Press, 2005.

Stein, R. Conrad. *World War II in Europe.* Berkeley Heights, N.J.: MyReportLinks.com Books, 2002.

———. *World War II in the Pacific.* Berkeley Heights, N.J.: MyReportLinks.com Books, 2002.

Warren, Andrea. *Surviving Hitler: A Boy in the Nazi Death Camps.* New York: HarperCollins Publishers, 2001.